ENTERPRISE COMPUTING SERIES

High Availability

Design, Techniques, and Processes

Floyd Piedad
Michael Hawkins

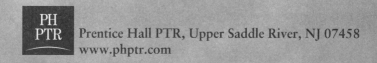

Prentice Hall PTR, Upper Saddle River, NJ 07458
www.phptr.com

Library of Congress Cataloging-in-Publication Data

CIP data available.

Editorial/Production Supervision: *Kathleen M. Caren*
Interior Compositor: *Vanessa Moore*
Acquisitions Editor: *Greg Doench*
Editorial Assistant: *Mary Treacy*
Marketing Manager: *Debby vanDijk*
Manufacturing Manager: *Alexis Heydt*
Cover Design Direction: *Jerry Votta*
Cover Design: *Talar Agasyan*
Series Design: *Gail Cocker-Bogusz*

© 2001 Prentice Hall PTR
Prentice-Hall, Inc.
Upper Saddle River, NJ 07458

Prentice Hall books are widely used by corporations and government agencies for training, marketing, and resale.

The publisher offers discounts on this book when ordered in bulk quantities.
For more information, contact:
Corporate Sales Department
Prentice Hall PTR
One Lake Street
Upper Saddle River, NJ 07458
Phone: 800-382-3419; fax: 201-236-7141; e-mail: corpsales@prenhall.com

Printed in the United States of America

10 9 8 7 6 5 4 3 2 1

ISBN 0-13-096288-0

Prentice-Hall International (UK) Limited, *London*
Prentice-Hall of Australia Pty. Limited, *Sydney*
Prentice-Hall Canada Inc., *Toronto*
Prentice-Hall Hispanoamericana, S.A., *Mexico*
Prentice-Hall of India Private Limited, *New Delhi*
Prentice-Hall of Japan, Inc., *Tokyo*
Pearson Education Asia Pte. Ltd.
Editora Prentice-Hall do Brasil, Ltda., *Rio de Janeiro*

Contents

Chapter 2

Achieving Higher Availability   13

Chapter 3

Planning for System Availability   25

Chapter 4

Preparing for Systems Management 31

Chapter 5

Implementing Service-Level Management 41

Chapter 6

From Centralized to Distributed Computing Environments   93

Chapter 10

Special Techniques for System Serviceability   189

Introduction

Back when the mainframe ruled the world, information technology (IT) practitioners quickly learned the value of a well-managed system. They understood the value of managing problems, changes, and other issues confronting large, mission-critical computer systems running an organization's most sensitive business functions.

When the popularity of mainframes waned in favor of less costly midrange and PC systems, IT organizations were caught in the frenzy of developing and deploying new business applications with breakneck speed. Suddenly, more computing power was available to end users, who wanted to accomplish more with it than ever before. The corporate information system grew in scope, use, and importance, with no end in sight.

Now that the dust has settled somewhat, both the IT organization and the leaders of the business recognize that an unmanaged state-of-the-art computer system can be as bad as having none at all. Symptoms of this problem with unmanaged systems manifest themselves in ballooning IT costs, overworked and demoralized IT staff, and user dissatisfaction.

This book demonstrates how to deliver maximum system availability and manageability throughout a computer system's lifecycle, from design through implementation and maintenance. We review every key technique for simplifying the management and maintenance of computer systems — including redundancy, standardization, backups, and many more. We discuss practical means of implementing these techniques to make your current and future systems far less prone to outages.

We cover technical and management issues, since you cannot achieve long-term system availability and manageability solutions without addressing both. We have written this book to benefit everyone in the IT organization. Technical staff will find practical operational solutions that can be implemented immediately. IT management will gain a better perspective of the end-to-end and interrelated requirements of running an IT shop. And Chief Information Officers (CIOs) and other senior IT executives will find forward-looking strategies for enhancing the IT infrastructure and its contribution to the corporate bottom line.

You can manage systems better if you design them with high systems availability in mind. This book will show you how to address *your* system availability problems, from start to finish.

Acknowledgments

To Harris Kern for his vision and insight.

To Grahame Khan, CEO, Khan & Hill, for his valuable knowledge and input.

To Ken Lee, Howie Lyke and the staff from Bluewater Information Convergence for their knowledge and insight. They truly understand the importance of designing for high availability.

To Victoria, Polo, Pia and Paola Piedad for being a source of inspiration.

To Sylvia, Kristle, Kurtis and Klifford Hawkins for their support and understanding.

Today's Computing Environment

▶ Complexity, Complexity, Complexity

Today more than ever, IT professionals are forced to operate in a complex business environment where success is no longer determined by a single factor, such as getting the best computer system or having the right technical skills. Now, complexity is the norm — and every aspect of the environment is becoming more complex. In the following sections, we identify six key areas of complexity.

Multiple Technologies and Protocols

Not long ago, mission-critical systems all ran on mainframe technology. With the advent of the PC, local area networks (LAN) and related technologies, many business applications moved from the protected realm of the mainframe data center to the free-flowing desktops of users.

At the host or central processing area, UNIX-based midrange computers and workstations arrived, handling scientific applications more gracefully, and serving as the breeding ground for the Internet. In place of mainframes, IT professionals can now choose specialized fault-tolerant or symmetric multiprocessing systems, or even low-end PC-based servers and workstations. Today's hottest gadgets include Palm PCs and other devices that connect to PCs and networks, allowing users to carry data in their pockets.

Once, if your system talked SNA, IBM's proprietary networking communication protocol, you could be understood by virtually all important systems and components. Today, you need to be fluent in TCP/IP and other protocols. Even your options for implementing networks can be overwhelming: Ethernet, Fast Ethernet, Gigabit Ethernet, ATM, ISDN, frame relay, xDSL, and many others.

Computing systems are no longer restricted to running on yesterday's computing platforms of choice: IBM's MVS or VSE. They may now run on UNIX, Linux, OS/400, Mac OS, Windows, OS/2, NetWare, Palm, Java-based devices, and many other alternative platforms. Even within these platform families, numerous versions and releases exist, and these are not necessarily compatible with each other. For example, UNIX has over 40 variants, even without counting the multiple distributions of Linux. Windows has Windows 3.1, Windows for Workgroups, Windows 95, Windows 98, Windows NT, Windows CE, and now Windows 2000 and Windows ME.

When dealing with the architecture or system deployment strategy, no longer are you bound to use host-based configurations where a large, powerful central computer does all the processing, and users interact via dumb terminals. In today's client-server architectures, each computing resource can be a client, a server, or both at different times. With this architecture, the mainframe is regarded as a fat server, and the dumb terminal becomes a thin client. Alternatively, you can choose a fat client (a powerful PC) that communicates with a thin server, or something in between — or a newer, Web-centered, or n-tier architecture. Each of these approaches presents unique deployment, management, and availability challenges.

Multiple Vendors

They say that the beauty of democracy is that everybody has freedom of choice. If so, nowhere is democracy practiced more fully than in the computer industry. You can buy from scores of vendors whose products implement the same popular technologies and standards, and safely assume that your products will work — *most* of the time, at least. Moreover, with the explosion in global electronic commerce, you can purchase software from anywhere on Earth, via the Internet, and download it directly from its authors. No longer are your choices limited to products sold by dealers and suppliers in your vicinity: you have direct access to the developers.

But freedom can be abused, and even in the best case, it creates enormous challenges for IT professionals, who are called upon to get multivendor products to work together with mission-critical reliability.

Varied Users

Technology is a great enabler, empowering individuals to perform equally well, wherever and whoever they are. Gone are the days when all requests for computations or data manipulation would have to be submitted to the data center. Today, nearly everyone in the organization has access to some computing resources.

Managers of every division can now access executive information systems, data warehouses, and corporate intranets for mission-critical decisions. Employees do most office-related work on PCs. Even contractual or temporary hires are provided at least limited access. And with the growth of the Internet and the proliferation of corporate web sites, customers can access the system for the latest product information or communicate with anybody in the organization via email.

As a result, IT professionals must ensure that their systems take into consideration the skills, experience, and language of a wider range of users than ever before.

Multiple Locations

With the growth of networks comes the challenge of managing computing resources that are physically distant from each other. In the 1960s, the IT organization only needed to worry about its "glass house" — the room where its giant mainframe was protected. Today, you must provide extensive remote user access. You can connect your system to the public telephone network, rent leased lines to remote departments or offices, even connect to the Internet. Your employees want to work from their homes, or from wherever their job takes them — to another building, city, province, or country. You must somehow manage these users also.

Rapid Change

Anybody who follows the information technology industry can attest to the fact that the rate of new product developments is exponentially growing. Companies once went several months without new product announcements. Now, not only do companies introduce new products (or versions of their products) more often, but many more companies are involved. A few years back, you could read back issues of two computer magazines and still be confident that what you were reading was current technology. Today, if you read an issue that's two months old, you know that what you're reading is well on its way to obsolescence. Web technologies such as HTML and XML rarely (or barely) reach full standardization before they are updated with newer versions.

Greater Business Demands

Information technology is no longer a matter of competitive advantage: it is a matter of survival. Your customers now routinely demand what were once "extra" features and capabilities. "What's your Web address so I can get more information about your products?" "Do you have an email address where I can send my problems or concerns?" "Can I do business with you electronically, and do away with all these paper forms?" "Can I access my bank account from the Internet?"

A Daunting Environment To Work In

To summarize, IT professionals are living in a world where they must deal with many different products from many different sources, deploying and managing them efficiently, to the satisfaction of a wide spectrum of possible users.

▶ The Total Cost of Ownership Issue

Many IT shops have discovered that large chunks of their costs have not been budgeted for properly. In response, consultants have come up with new Total Cost of Ownership (TCO) models for accurately costing today's distributed computing systems, and for reflecting previously unbudgeted expenses.

Total Cost of Ownership Defined

The TCO of a computing system is an organization's total cost for acquiring *and maintaining* that system.

Once, many IT professionals only factored in the costs of purchasing hardware and applications. This wasn't surprising: they grew up in the relatively easy-to-manage world of mainframes, where these were, by far, the most important costs to consider. Now, however, in the era of e-business, PCs and client-server systems, the amount of work needed to *manage and maintain* systems has become overwhelming.

End users cannot be blamed for taking it upon themselves to deploy departmental applications, when a few years ago they could not get their mainframe gurus to deliver solutions quickly enough. But now that these systems are in place, there are more components, locations, and users to manage — and the costs of computing now go far beyond the costs of acquisition.

What should go into the computation of the TCO of any system?

- **Acquisition cost** comprises the cost of acquiring the system, and includes the costs to:
  - **Research** possible products to buy
  - **Design** the system and all the necessary components to ensure that they work well together
  - **Source** the products, which means getting the best possible deal from all the possible vendors
  - **Purchase** the products — the selling price as negotiated with the chosen supplier
  - **Install** the system
  - **Develop** or customize the applications to be used

- **Train** the users
- **Deploy** the system, including transitioning existing business processes

- **Cost of maintaining availability** of the system to the end users, which covers:
  - **Systems management,** including every aspect of maintaining normal operations, such as activation and shutdown, job control, output management, backup and recovery.
  - **Maintenance of hardware and software components,** including preventive and corrective maintenance, and housekeeping.
  - **User support,** including ongoing training, help desk facilities, and problem support.
  - **Environmental factors,** a system's external requirements for proper operation, such as air conditioning, power supply, housing, and floor space.
  - **Other factors** that do not fall in any of the above categories, depending on the type of system deployed and the prevailing circumstances.

All these seem straightforward, but quantifying each cost is difficult if not impractical in today's world, because few organizations have an accounting practice that is mature enough to break down expenses in sufficient detail.

For example, we know of no organization that records all employee activities by task, information you would need to answer questions like these: *What support costs did you incur last month? How much time did each user spend in solving computer-related problems? How much work was lost due to downtime on desktop PCs?*

Additionally, companies rarely have accurate inventory and asset information regarding their computing systems, especially in large, distributed computing environments where PC, server and LAN purchasing decisions are often handled locally.

So, what's the value of knowing a system's TCO? Obviously, our objective is not to calculate exact figures. Rather, you need to understand what these costs *could reasonably be* in your organization. You must plan for these costs, even if you can only roughly estimate them. The TCO also provides a good basis of comparison between alternative system deployment strategies, between platforms, and between competing products.

Industry TCO Estimates

When IT and user labor costs are factored in, industry consultants have estimated the TCO of typical office PC systems at roughly $10,000 per unit, *per year.* Compare this with the typical PC system cost of around $1,500, and you can see that the hardware and software costs account for only 15 percent of the total cost of ownership.

TCO computations for other system configurations for distributed network computing agree: hardware and software costs account for only a small portion of the total cost of ownership of *any* contemporary system. As you provide more functionality and capability to end users, TCO rises. As you install more software or provide more complex hardware, you pay increasingly more for support and maintenance.

As you can see, TCO provides a good model for evaluating computing costs — visible and invisible, budgeted and unbudgeted. We do not say that TCO should be your sole determining factor for choosing a system. However, you should be aware of these costs and plan for them. You must always balance the costs of providing a system versus the benefits to the business.

What TCO Studies Reveal

TCO studies of PCs have identified several key hidden, unbudgeted costs:

- **Fiddle factor** — Users often spend excessive time changing minor look-and-feel items on their PCs — time that could be spent performing productive work. Examples are: changing how the Windows desktop looks (e.g., color, size, icons, screensavers); installing applets or utilities (e.g., pop-up messages, animated cursors, desktop accessories); and trying out different fonts or lettering styles in documents. These activities can distract users from the more important task of ensuring quality content.

- **Peer support and self-help phenomenon** — When end users encounter problems, they rarely seek IT help. They either try to solve the problem on their own, or ask colleagues to assist, taking coworkers away from their primary job responsibilities. Not only that, as users try to gain as much computer expertise as possible, they often neglect the skills they need in their line of work. Most of their computer expertise is learned informally, by time-consuming experimentation that often causes even more complex problems.

- **User-introduced problems** — Often, users themselves cause unnecessary downtime and lost productivity through their own activities:

  - Deleting critical system files by accident or experiment

  - Changing parameters in the Windows system registry or control panel

  - Installing new software that causes incompatibilities or virus infections

  - Installing counterproductive software (e.g., games)

Problem areas in distributed client-server environments include the following:

- **Problem support** — Users need access to quality support on a timely basis. Most users revert to peer support or self-support when they cannot get the level of assistance they need. The IT organization typically fails for the following reasons:

  - It is unreachable or too distant (not necessarily physically) from users

  - It did not publicize who to contact for what types of problems

  - It does not know how to support the user's configuration (common in those systems where the users bought the systems on their own)

  - It does know how to support remote servers and distributed networks

  - It takes too long to solve user problems

  - It has no time to deal with end-user problems

- **Inventory management and control** — Often, the IT organization cannot track the configuration of most of the systems in use, especially in large organizations. When you factor in systems installed in remote locations or used by telecommuters, the situation can become even more chaotic. In order to plan for, and deliver quality user support and asset management, IT organizations must *at minimum* know the number of units installed, who owns each system, and each system's hardware and software configuration.

- **Software configuration and update management** — IT organizations are called upon to install hardware or software upgrades to systems efficiently and in a timely manner — and PC software gets updated often. There must be a way to make updates remotely, without visiting every server and desktop. There must also be a mechanism for controlling configuration files on user workstations and regulating the installation or modification of software. These requirements were never a concern back in the mainframe-centric world, as all applications were stored and run from the central host.

The Underlying Reason for High TCO

Where a company's systems have especially high TCO, its systems were most likely deployed with only the following issues in mind:

- **Functionality** — The capability of a computer to perform the tasks and run the applications required by the user.

- **Performance** — The capability of a computer to respond to user input as quickly as possible (often referred to as *system response time*).

- **Capacity** — The capability to handle growth in concurrent users, amount of data processed, number of transactions completed, or other metrics.

After the systems were deployed, issues not directly related to these criteria cropped up — issues that proved every bit as important to users over the long term. These *post-deployment requirements* include:

- **Availability** — The system or application is there when the user needs it
- **Ease of use** — No complicated procedures to learn or remember
- **Assistance** — If the user has a problem, help is easily accessible
- **Security** — The user's work is protected from loss or unauthorized access

In all cases where the TCO of a system is unnecessarily high, it is because the system or application was designed without taking into consideration the post-deployment user requirements above, particularly: availability, security, and assistance.

A Typical Scenario: Choosing Office Systems

Here's an example of how inattention to post-deployment requirements can lead to high TCO. In most large companies, the decision to purchase PCs and client-server systems is often delegated to departments, often without any guidelines from the IT organization. Users (and most young IT organizations), unaware of the need to consider post-deployment requirements, make choices based solely on functionality, performance, capacity, and price.

Given the maturity of PC and server technology and the relatively stable standards in designing LANs today, almost any hardware can qualify. As a result, inexperienced purchasers often choose unbranded systems sold at lower prices, rather than brand-name systems made by vendors such as Sun, IBM, Compaq, and Dell.

Retailers typically assemble unbranded computers using components sourced from multiple manufacturers. Unfortunately, these systems often suffer from poor quality control. Purchasers are likely to encounter unknown bugs because of substandard design or assembly; high failures due to poor quality components; poor after-sales support; and little or no system documentation. Having disregarded post-deployment requirements, they end up paying more for:

- **Support** — IT organizations must develop their own expertise since they cannot rely on the retailer, and they may have to spend more time researching problem resolution. One company spent a sizable amount simply searching for current software patches, hardware drivers, and BIOS tuning parameters. Even so, they could not get the same level of performance as branded computers with comparable hardware and software configurations.

- **Lost user productivity** — If a system intermittently fails, or if other problems occur, system downtime can be far longer than normal.

- **Repairs** — Because warranties may not be clearly documented, and retailers often blamed problems on users, IT organizations often find themselves replacing suspicious components simply to avoid hassles.

- **System security** — Most unbranded computers have no means to prevent access inside the casing; most well designed branded computers have locks or other security mechanisms. One company we encountered had problems with missing memory chips they suspected were being stolen by employees for use in home computers.

Availability as the Most Significant Contributor to TCO

Our experience with information systems has shown us that the user requirement responsible for the greatest hidden costs is *availability*. This user requirement takes precedence over all others. What good is a system if it is unavailable? It also requires ongoing management and maintenance throughout the entire life of every system.

A system is available when users can work with it without experiencing outages. Note that for as long as the user does not perceive or feel the outage, the system is available to him. Availability is measured from the user's point of view. A user will consider a system unavailable if:

- **The system is not accessible** — If the users cannot access the resources they need to run their application, the system is unavailable. The system is equally unavailable if all workstations or software licenses are in use, or if the network connection to necessary data is down, or if the system has a virus infection.

- **The system is running too slow** — The system may be operational but if the response time is long, the user will give up waiting and consider the system as unavailable.
- **The system is intermittently having problems** — The user will choose not to use a system if she suspects her work may be lost due to intermittent system failures.

Summary

In today's client-server-dominated IT environment, we must understand TCO in order to effectively evaluate all of our deployment alternatives. All studies on TCO have shown that the TCO of interconnected servers and workstations is high compared to the centralized mainframe and dumb terminals of yesteryear, and the key reason is inattention to post-deployment requirements, especially availability.

Availability deals not only with the prevention of "real" system outages, but with user-perceived outages as well. These perceived outages are anything that prevents the user from working with the system productively, such as prolonged response times, lack of assistance, or lack of available workstations.

We can slash TCO by designing systems and applications with availability in mind. In the next section, we will review availability requirements in greater detail, in order to properly address them.

Achieving Higher Availability

▶ Determining User Availability Requirements

The first step in designing for availability is to discover your users' true requirements for availability — and for IT services in general. This requires close consultation with as many users as possible, covering at least users of critical applications. The initial response of most users is that the system must be available *all* the time. Of course, you need to explain that the cost for providing system availability gets higher and higher as more availability is needed. You'll also need to explain that these costs will be passed on to them somehow — either *directly*, as IT chargeback for services, or (as in most small-to-mid-sized companies) *indirectly*, as the IT organization takes a larger share of the corporate budget.

The Service Level Agreement

These consultations with users form the basis of a Service Level Agreement between the provider of IT services and the users. You can choose to limit yourselves to a simple agreement that covers just system availability, or you can expand the agreement to include response time, help desk availability, new feature request turnaround time, and many other performance and quality issues. If you are starting from scratch, we recommend including just the system availability portion. Then, as the system becomes more stable and your IT organization matures, you can expand on that agreement. This approach has many benefits:

- **The users do not expect too much too soon** — The final judges of the IT organization's performance are the users, so it is crucial to manage their expectations.
- **It buys the IT organization time to improve on services** — This is an opportunity for the IT organization to be one step ahead of user requirements. It gives the organization a better feel for the resource demands associated with meeting availability requirements, and allows for better planning.
- **It allows for a less demanding agreement** — Since users know that the agreement will be improved later, they will be more willing to settle for a realistic short-term target.

Never commit what you know you cannot achieve. Agree on a target you can truly achieve in the short term, and establish a timetable for achieving higher system availability in the future. First, pilot the system availability target internally within the IT organization or with one small department. Once you've demonstrated that you can meet your target, roll out the new service level standards throughout the rest of the organization.

Helping Users Identify Their Availability Requirements

The first questions to ask users are:

> **What are your scheduled operations? What times of the day and days of the week do you expect to be using the system or application?**

The answers help you identify times your system or application must be available. Normally, the responses coincide with the users' regular working hours. For example, users may primarily work with an application from 8:00 a.m. to 5:00 p.m. from Mondays to Fridays. However, some users want to be able to access the system for overtime work. Depending on the number of users who access the system during off hours, you can choose to include those times in your normal operating hours. Alternatively, you can set up a procedure for users to request off-hours system availability at least three days in advance.

When external users or customers access a system, its operating hours are often extended well beyond the normal business hours. This is especially true with online banking, Internet services, e-commerce systems and other essential utilities such as electricity, water, and communications. Users of these systems usually demand availability 24 hours a day, 7 days a week, or as close as possible.

The second set of questions to ask users is:

How often can you tolerate system outages during the times that you are using the system or application? How about scheduled outages?

Your goal is to understand the impact on users if the system becomes unavailable when it is scheduled to be available. For example, a user may say that he can only afford two outages a month.

This answer also tells you if you can ever schedule an outage during times when the system is committed to be available. You may wish to do so for maintenance, upgrades, or other housekeeping purposes. For instance, a system that should be on line 24 hours a day, 7 days a week may still require a scheduled downtime at midnight to perform full backups.

The final question to ask users is:

How long can an outage last if one does occur?

This question helps identify how long the user is willing to wait for the restoration of the system during an outage, or to what extent the outages can be tolerated without severely impacting the business. For example, a user may say that any outage can only last for up to a maximum of three hours. Often, a user will be able to tolerate outages longer if they are scheduled.

▶ Availability Levels and Measurements

Based on the answers to the questions discussed in the previous section, we can specify which category of availability your users require:

- **High availability** — System or application is available during specified operating hours with no unplanned outages.
- **Continuous operations** — System or application is available 24 hours a day, 7 days a week with no scheduled outages.
- **Continuous availability** — System or application is available 24 hours a day, 7 days a week with no planned or unplanned outages.

High Availability Level

High availability is the level of availability normally expected by users. At this level, once you commit to a schedule of system availability, there should be *no* unscheduled or unplanned outages or downtimes. For example, the system is committed to be available from 8:00 a.m. to 5:00 p.m. from Monday to Friday. There should be no unplanned outages during this time. Any outage would definitely impact users since they could be in the middle of important work.

Is an outage pre-announced or not? Remember whose perspective matters — *the user's.* If you announce an outage an hour in advance, you might consider it planned, but your users may consider it unplanned, since they don't have enough time to adjust their work to cope with it.

When the outage will occur and when the users are informed about it are both important. For example, telling the users at 8:00 a.m. that a downtime will occur in eight hours is more acceptable than telling them at 5 p.m. that an outage will happen at 8:00 a.m. the following day, since the latter example gives users no time to prepare, unless they work overtime.

High availability still gives you room to schedule system downtimes, as long as you schedule them outside the committed availability period. For example, you can deliver high availability while retaining the ability to schedule nightly backups. You must, however, ensure that the system operates reliably during committed periods of availability. The challenge here is to eliminate problems, or at least make them transparent to users or less likely to affect system availability.

Continuous Operations Level

Continuous operations means a system is committed to constant availability, with no unscheduled *or* scheduled downtime. To achieve this level, you must implement high availability and continuous operations techniques that make the system more reliable and eliminate dependence on scheduled maintenance work that would require system downtime.

Continuous Availability

At the *continuous availability* level, the system is committed to be available always, with no scheduled and unscheduled operations. To achieve this, you must implement high availability and continuous operations techniques to make the system more reliable and not dependent on scheduled maintenance work requiring system downtime.

This level of availability is normally demanded in critical systems that provide essential services to the general public, such as electricity, communication systems, and banking services such as Automated Teller Machines (ATMs). Internet service providers and e-commerce systems also need continuous availability. Obviously, this level of availability is the hardest and most costly to achieve. Users must be aware of this expense, and must be willing to pay for it. One hundred percent continuous availability is almost impossible to achieve consistently.

Quantifying Availability Targets

To quantify the amount of availability achieved, we must calculate:

- **Committed hours of availability (A)** — Usually measured in terms of number of hours per month or any other period suitable to your organization.

  Example: 24 hours a day, 7 days a week = 24 hours per day × 7 days = 720 hours per month

- **Outage hours (B)** — Number of hours of outage during the committed hours of availability. If the availability level is high availability, then consider only those unplanned outages. For continuous operations, consider only those scheduled outages. But for continuous availability, consider all outages.

Example: Nine hours of outage due to hard disk crash, 15 hours of outage due to preventive maintenance

Then, for our example, we calculate the amount of availability achieved as follows:

Achieved availability = ((A – B)/A) × 100 percent)

Example:
High availability = ((720 – 15)/720) × 100 percent = 97.92 percent
Continuous Operations = ((720 – 9)/720) × 100 percent = 98.75 percent
Continuous availability = ((720 – 24)/720) × 100 percent = 96.67 percent

When negotiating an availability target with users, make them aware of its implications. Here is a table of availability targets versus hours of outage allowed for a continuous availability level requirement.

Continuous Availability Target	Hours of Outage Per Month Allowed
99.99 percent	0.07 hours
99.9 percent	0.7 hours
99.5 percent	3.6 hours
99.0 percent	7.2 hours
98.6 percent	10.0 hours
98.0 percent	14.4 hours

Recognize that numbers like these are difficult to achieve, since time is needed to recover from outages. The length of recovery time correlates with:

- **Complexity of the system** — The more complicated your system is, the longer it takes to restart it. Hence, outages that require system shutdown and restart can dramatically impact your ability to meet a challenging availability target. For example, applications running on a large server can take up to an hour just to restart when the system was shut down normally, longer still if the system had been abnormally terminated and data files had to be recovered.

- **Severity of the problem** — Usually, the greater the severity of the problem, the more time is needed to fully resolve the problem, including restoring lost data or work done.

- **Availability of support personnel** — Let's say the outage occurs after office hours. A support person called in after hours could easily take an hour or two simply to arrive to diagnose the problem. You must allow for this possibility.

- **Other factors** — Many other factors prevent the immediate resolution of an outage. Sometimes an application may have an extended outage simply because the system cannot be put offline because other applications are running. Other cases involve the lack of replacement hardware by the system supplier, or even lack of support staff. We have seen many availability targets missed simply because a system supplier could not give due attention to the problem, and no backup system supplier existed.

Availability: A User Metric

Again, keep in mind that availability is measured from *the user's point of view*. A system is available if the user can use the application he needs. Otherwise, it is unavailable. Accordingly, availability must be measured *end-to-end*. All components needed to run the application are available. Many IT organizations mistakenly believe that availability is simply equal to main server or network availability. Some may only measure the availability of critical system components. These are grave mistakes. A user may equally be prevented from using an application because his PC is broken, or his data is unavailable, or his PC is infected with a computer virus.

IT organizations that subscribe to a narrow or undisciplined availability mindset go through several stages of alienation from their users.

User unhappiness is the first and least severe stage. Users simply express unhappiness with poor system availability. The IT organization may either recognize a problem or deny it, citing their host or network availability statistics as proof. Those who deny the problem's existence bring their organization to the next stage of user alienation.

User distrust is characterized by user disbelief in much of what the IT organization says. Users may begin to view IT's action plans as insufficient, or view the IT organization as incapable of implementing its plans. They gradually lose interest in helping IT with end user surveys and consultations. IT organizations that can deliver on promises and provide better availability *from the user's point of view* can prevent users from moving to the next stage of user alienation.

User opposition is the third stage of alienation. Here, users do not merely ignore IT plans. They begin to actively oppose them, suggesting alternatives that may not align with IT's overall plans. Users start to take matters into their own hands, researching alternatives that might help solve their problems. The challenge for the IT organization is to convince users that the IT plan is superior. The best way to meet this challenge is to conduct a pilot test of the user's suggested alternative, then evaluate the results hand-in-hand with users. In contrast, we have seen some IT organizations react arrogantly, telling users to "do what you want, but don't come crying to us for help." These organizations find themselves facing the final stage of user alienation.

User outsourcing is the final stage of user alienation. Users convince management that the best solution lies outside the IT organization. Outsourcing can take the form of hiring an outside consultant to design their system, going directly to an outside system supplier, or even setting up their own IT organization. At this stage, users have completely broken off from the IT organization, and reduced — if not totally eliminated — the need to fund it.

Beyond user alienation, there are other serious side effects of insisting on narrow-minded availability measurement.

- **Failure to identify root causes of availability problems** — If only a few components are considered when system availability is evaluated, the root causes of the outages may well lie in components whose availability is not monitored. We have seen several banking IT organizations that have denied the existence of Automated Teller Machine problems by pointing out that their mainframes, switches, and network are always available. They fail to observe that the ATM machines themselves cause most ATM outages.

- **Conflicts between IT divisions** — Many IT organizations usually delegate critical elements of their systems to individual groups within IT. Each then measures the availability of its assigned area, without correlating it with the availability of other areas. This leads to territorial disputes where one group blames others for poor system availability. "Don't blame my group! Our network was up 100 percent of the time..."

- **Expensive and ineffective remedial measures** — If you do not know what the root cause of a problem is, you'll probably spend money on the wrong solution. Or, you'll concentrate on improving only *your* assigned system component, without regard to overall system availability.

- **Inability to determine true system health** — Availability measurements of each component cannot easily be "added up" to reveal true system availability. Ninety-nine percent host availability + 99 percent network availability + 99 percent database availability is not equal to 99 percent system availability. Outages in each area usually occur at different times, and each outage in any component brings the entire system down. In this example, actual system availability can be anywhere from 97 percent to 99 percent.

Why do many IT organizations fall into the trap of measuring only a few system components and not actual end-to-end availability? There are two reasons.

First, it is easier to measure a few system components. Few tools are available for analyzing and monitoring end-to-end system availability. Many tools measure network or host availability, but few actually check for application outages from the perspective of the user. Second, it is easier to achieve higher availability on a per component basis since outages rarely occur repeatedly on the same component. Outages for different components usually occur at different times but may all affect the availability of the system to the user, resulting in far worse availability statistics.

Measuring End-To-End Availability

To accurately estimate end-to-end application availability as experienced by end users, you must first thoroughly understand the system's configuration; all the components and resources used by the application, both local and remote; and the hardware and software components required to access those resources. Here is an example:

Sales Personnel Call Management System

Local resources	Sales personnel data Call reports
Remote resources	Contact management data at each sales rep's computer
Hardware components	Personal computer, LAN adapter, LAN cabling, network switch, print server, network printer
Software components	Windows 98, MS Access, contact management software, call management application

The next step is to monitor all these components for outages. If outages are detected on multiple components at the same time, treat the outage duration as just one instance. To calculate end-to-end availability, add all the outages of each component. Then, apply the formula presented earlier in this chapter.

Sounds easy in principle, but taxing in practice? Definitely. That's why you need to automate measurement as much as possible. The simplest way is to use a tool that monitors availability of local and remote resources from a user's PC. This tool regularly attempts to get a response from the resources in question, and records times that critical resources are unavailable. More advanced tools can query an application for problems or execute certain tasks on the application. If the application fails, an outage is recorded. This approach does not identify the source of the problem, but the error condition may help support staffers identify the cause.

There is a great demand for automated end user system availability monitoring tools — utilities that can be installed in user workstations that would periodically test the applications for availability. In the absence of such tools, you would have to resort to random sampling of users' availability experiences.

You won't get precise measurements of every user's availability experience. That's unrealistic. Do, however, recognize that users have an availability requirement you must pay attention to. Don't get too dependent on technical measurements for rating your performance. Ultimately, what matters most is that users are happy with the service that the IT organization provides.

Remember that the discussion in this section focuses on how availability is affected by hardware or software outages. Again, this is not the only factor by which a user judges system availability. The system may not be experiencing an outage, but if it is running too slowly, a user may give up waiting and consider an application unavailable. Hardware and software outages, though, make up the majority of the reasons for unavailability.

▶ Summary

IT must understand the level of availability users require, and users must understand the costs of achieving these targets. Often, IT loses users' trust and confidence by dictating availability targets without proper consultation. Conversely, users often make unrealistic demands on IT, failing to recognize the cost implications.

Of all availability levels, continuous availability is the most challenging and expensive to provide. More often than not, users are willing to settle for high availability but with committed hours of operations as close as possible to 24 hours a day, 7 days a week.

Availability is a user metric, which means that we must measure it from the point of view of the user's experience. Most IT organizations that lose the support of their users have failed to recognize this, focusing instead on the availability of only a few critical components.

Planning for System Availability

▶ Identifying System Components

To improve system availability, first identify all the system components that work together to enable a user's application to run. A chain is only as strong as its weakest link. If your system has one component that is prone to failure, your entire system is prone to failure.

Most systems can be divided into the following elements:

- **Host or server** — This is the portion of the system where most data is stored or processed. The server fulfills transaction requests sent to it and sends the results to the requestor of the transaction. For example, in a bank Automated Teller Machine (ATM) system, the host is usually the bank mainframe system, or large server, that manages client bank accounts and transactions.
- **Client** — This is the component that makes a request from the server. In our ATM example, the client is the ATM machine.
- **Network** — This is the component that allows the client to communicate with the server, and vice versa. In our ATM example, the network is typically a combination of a private network, the public telephone network and all associated communication equipment.

25

For each of these areas, examine all components: hardware, software, environment, processes and procedures, and personnel.

Hardware is the physical equipment making up the system. It includes, but is not limited to, the following:

- **Central processing unit** — The device that controls the operation of the computer system or other intelligent equipment

- **Storage devices** — Data repositories, whether permanent or volatile media, such as memory and hard disks

- **Input devices** — Components for receiving commands or data from users or other equipment, for example, keyboards, mice, and serial ports

- **Output devices** — Components for presenting data to the user, such as monitors, speakers, and printers

- **Cables** — Often neglected but crucial to the reliability of any computer system

Software consists of the programs running in the system that enable it to perform its functions, including:

- **Firmware** — Software embedded in hardware, acting as the interface between hardware resources and the operating system. In PCs, this software is also called the Basic Input/Output System (BIOS).

- **Operating system** — Core programs that allow applications to run on a computer without directly interfacing with the computer's hardware components. Common operating systems include Windows 95/98, Windows 2000, UNIX, Linux, OS/400 and OS/390.

- **Utilities** — Software that performs housekeeping and system control functions. Normally, system administrators or maintenance staffers use these programs.

- **Programming software** — Software that supports the creation of applications, including languages such as C++, Java and COBOL, and development tools such as Microsoft Visual Studio.

- **Applications** — Programs designed to perform user-specified tasks or operations. These programs may be written by the company (in-house applications) or purchased from a software vendor (off-the-shelf or shrink-wrapped software).

- **Middleware** — Programs supporting communication or data exchange between multiple programs or computer systems.

Environment is the external equipment the system needs in order to run:

- **Power** — Including automatic voltage regulators, uninterruptible power supplies, generators, surge suppressors, and lightning arrestors
- **Cooling** — Including air conditioning units and dehumidifiers
- **Floor space** — Including raised flooring and secured access areas

Processes and procedures are the operational activities needed to run the system. These include, but are not limited to:

- **Activation** — Including power up, system initialization, application startup, and verification of system activation
- **Operation** — Including resource management, input/output control, job control, and network management
- **Systems management** — Including system monitoring and change administration
- **Housekeeping** — Including backup and restore, as well as archiving of data
- **User management** — Including user and security administration
- **Deactivation** — Including application shutdown, system shutdown, and power down

People refers to those who interact with the system:

- **Users** — Including both internal and external users
- **System support staff** — Including operators, system administrators, programmers, technical support professionals, and others
- **Vendors and suppliers** — Including electricity vendors, equipment suppliers, telecommunications providers, and others

Addressing Critical Components

After you identify all relevant system components, the next step is to find the *critical* system components, those that represent single points of failure for the system. When these components encounter a problem, the entire system is affected.

Several approaches are available for reducing the risks associated with these critical components:

- **Reduce outage frequency** — Look for ways to prevent outages from happening to that critical component, thereby increasing its reliability.
- **Minimize outage duration** — If outages cannot be entirely avoided, find ways to recover immediately from them, thereby improving recoverability. If recovery is impossible, ensure that the component can be immediately repaired. In other words, improve serviceability.
- **Minimize outage scope** — Minimize the parts of a system that are impacted by an outage.
- **Prevent future outages** — Reduce the potential for users and other external factors to affect system availability, and make it easier to maintain the system's health by addressing its *manageability*.

The Four Elements of Availability

From the preceding section, we can define four elements of availability:

- **Reliability** — The ability to perform under stated conditions for a stated period of time
- **Recoverability** — The ability to easily bypass and recover from a component failure
- **Serviceability** — The ability to perform effective problem determination, diagnosis, and repair
- **Manageability** — The ability to create and maintain an environment that limits the negative impact people may have on the system

▶ Summary

To devise an effective plan to address system availability, you must first understand the *entire* system, and how each component affects overall system availability. By then identifying the *most critical* system components, you can intelligently set priorities. Remember that no matter how insignificant a system component may seem, it can have a profound effect on overall system availability. Once you identify the most critical components, seek ways to improve their *reliability, recoverability, serviceability,* and *manageability*.

Next, we review the IT discipline with the greatest impact on system availability — the often-neglected discipline of systems management.

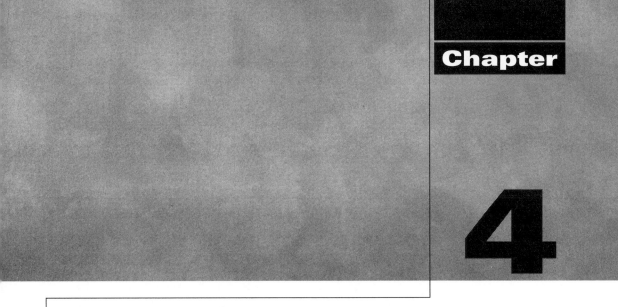

Preparing for Systems Management

▶ Processes, Data, Tools, and Organization

Systems Management is the combination of processes, data, tools, and organization needed to manage a system efficiently and effectively. *Processes* deal with how to perform the task. *Data* refers to the information required to perform the process. *Tools* are the equipment needed to perform the processes. *Organization* refers to the people that support the process and how they are set up to do so.

Systems management is not merely a set of procedures for running a system, rather, it integrates all four elements mentioned above. We have seen too many IT organizations come up with exhaustively detailed procedures, yet fail because they have not tackled all four key elements.

To illustrate, let us review examples of implementations that lacked one or more of these elements:

- **Process element ignored** — Many help desks have no escalation procedures. Obviously, this leads to many complaints by users (and their management), when severe problems do not receive

31

appropriate attention and support. To add insult to injury, in many cases, IT management only becomes aware of these problems when users complain.

- **Data element ignored** — Often, help desks fail to adequately identify the data they need to gather from users. One help desk had more-than-adequate staffing, and clear procedures for handling calls. However, nobody quite knew what information to request, and there was no standard form for recording details. Whenever the caller's problem was passed to technical support, the support person usually had to call the user again for more information. Problem resolution was delayed, productivity suffered, and users were dissatisfied. Eventually, users decided that calling the centralized help desk was a waste of time, and began calling support specialists directly.

- **Tools element ignored** — This is the most common systems management mistake IT organizations make — they erroneously believe you can simply throw bodies at the problem. One organization's help desk was in total disarray because the help desk staff was demoralized. We discovered they had no computerized means of recording and tracking calls — they were simply using a paper-based logbook. When management asked for weekly reports, the help desk staff needed a whole day simply to sort and filter their call records. Adding staff simply led to more paper shuffling, and even more lost call information.

- **Organization element ignored** — Many IT organizations seem to think that you can have an effective help desk simply by seating people in front of a phone to answer user calls. They fail to recognize that it is also important to *organize* the people making up the help desk. Organizing a help desk includes identifying the appropriate staffing and skills requirements, creating clear reporting lines within the help desk organization, and distributing responsibilities efficiently amongst the help desk staff. Without the right people *and* the proper organizational structure, there is little chance that calls will be handled properly. Moreover, there may be little cooperation among the help desk staff. Calls will most likely pass from one person to another without ever getting resolved adequately.

Systems Management in the PC World (or the Lack of It)

Systems management covers all aspects of an IT operation, from design and procurement of IT equipment to its implementation, problem resolution, security, and much more. No matter how small your computing resource, you need some form of systems management discipline in order to preserve system availability and maximize IT's value to your business. Systems management may have evolved in the mainframe environment, but even a single PC can benefit from well-implemented systems management techniques.

Consider your typical standalone PC. How many times did you have to reinstall your operating system because you installed new software that changed system configuration files — and degraded the entire system? If you had implemented even just the basic change management practice of creating a backup copy of system configuration files before making changes, you could have easily undone the changes and restored your system to health. Newer operating systems (notably Windows 2000) incorporate features that help protect configuration files from unauthorized change. Upgrading to these operating systems may be worth serious consideration.

IT Organizations: Away from Centralization, Then Back Again

In the continuing wave of migration from mainframe-centric systems to distributed client-server systems, users have initiated most of the migration. These users became fed up with the slow pace at which mainframe shops delivered new applications. In the client-server world, they found many off-the-shelf software packages, tools for faster, easier applications development; and lower upfront hardware and software costs. Unsurprisingly, they began making their own purchasing decisions, disregarding centralized IT organizations.

As these new distributed systems have matured and grown, businesses have become extremely dependent on them. Gradually, small problems — which users could easily deal with — grew in number and complexity. Users without experience running mission-critical systems were faced with managing database backups, optimizing performance, supporting large numbers of users, and many other difficult challenges. What was easy to deploy and manage became extremely difficult to maintain and control. Increasingly, users are willingly relinquishing control of their client-server-based systems to centralized IT organizations that "know more about managing these systems than we do."

The lesson is simple — having the right hardware or software does not guarantee that you will always have the system you need. You must consciously plan your system, and diligently manage it. Hence, the need for systems management disciplines.

▶ ## Understanding the Systems To Manage

To deploy the optimal systems management infrastructure, you must first thoroughly understand the system you intend to manage. Knowing the technical aspects of your system is not enough. To design a cost-effective, practical systems management infrastructure, consider the following points:

- **How critical the system is to the business** — Greater criticality requires better systems management. Consider how much of the business will be affected if the system is not available, in terms of lost productivity, increased expenses, lost business opportunities, and erosion of customer satisfaction.

- **Size of the system to manage** — Expect your systems management infrastructure to be increasingly complex as system size increases. Size can be gauged in terms of the amount of resources (hardware, software, people, etc.) being utilized, the amount of data being processed, or the number of users being served.

- **Complexity of the system** — The more complex a system, the more difficult it is to manage. Complexity is a measure of the number of different resources interacting and working with each other. A system can be complex for many reasons. For example, it may be complex because multiple operating systems are in use, or because many types of users are sharing the same set of applications (e.g., customers, suppliers, managers, and staff). When multiple components are shared, there is greater risk of dysfunction or reduced performance due to competition for scarce resources.

- **Distribution of system components across different locations** — Increasingly, components are distributed across servers and workstations in different buildings, cities, or even countries. Components that are widely dispersed are more difficult to manage effectively. System management processes associated with dispersed components are likely to be slower and more prone to failures.

- **Ownership of resources** — It becomes more difficult to coordinate systems if many different owners have the final say as to what is done, simply because you must get permission from many different people and coordinate all their decisions and actions. In a highly distributed computing environment, it is common to have different owners for the workstations, servers, communication facilities (often owned by a telecommunications company or service provider), and many others.

- **Security requirements** — Systems and information assets that must be protected introduce new complexities, such as access control and authentication, making them more difficult to manage.

- **Skill sets** — When devising a systems management infrastructure, consider not only the skills of the IT organization, but also those of users. As systems become increasingly distributed, management responsibilities may also be distributed, and everyone involved is likely to need new skills and training.

- **New technologies** — Consider forthcoming technologies and your organization's long term IT goals, so the systems management infrastructure you design will not be made obsolete by rapid change.

- **Environmental dependencies** — It may be difficult or impossible to control the external environment in which your systems operate, but you can limit the impact of changes in the external environment on the operations of your systems. For example, if the power supplied to your equipment is prone to outages, you can deploy backup power generation facilities and establish procedures for switching to them.

- **Standards** — You cannot deploy the right tools without considering corporate hardware and software standardization policies. Also consider company operations rules, such as security guidelines and employee management standards.

▶ The Basics of Management: Five Phases

The traditional formula for effective systems management of any system, process, or activity comprises five phases. These phases were identified based upon close examination of the key issues faced by managers:

- What activities must be performed everyday?
- How do we know these get done when they're supposed to?
- Who is responsible for performing each activity?
- How do we know if it's being done effectively and efficiently?
- Who tells management how it's going?
- Who gets blamed if things don't go right?
- How can you improve what you're doing?

The five phases of management activity related to systems management are described in the following sections.

Phase 1: Setting Objectives

The first and most important phase is setting objectives. Here, we determine the requirements of the business and end users. Without properly determining what needs to be achieved, it is nearly impossible to execute the other phases effectively. You must understand user objectives, so your plans and activities support them.

Alice in Wonderland provides a wonderful lesson. Lost in the forest, Alice came upon a fork in the road and asked the Cheshire Cat which road to take. The Cheshire Cat's answer, in paraphrase:

"It does not matter which road you take if you don't know where you are going."

In mature IT organizations, setting objectives often takes the form of defining Service Level Agreements — enumerating the different services to be provided to the users, and corresponding attributes such as performance, availability, and features.

Phase 2: Planning

In the planning phase, based on the objectives determined above, you define a plan to meet those objectives. This plan usually covers the resources to be deployed, the activities to be done, the measurements to be tracked, the tools to be used, and how the people are to be organized. Again, we cannot overemphasize the need to address the four elements of systems management: *process, data, tools,* and *organization.*

Phase 3: Execution

In the execution phase, we actually perform the steps that were planned in Phase 2.

Phase 4: Measurement

In this phase, we record relevant data regarding the execution of the plan. Many different measures can be tracked, falling into categories such as *performance* (speed of execution of a task), *capacity* (number of concurrent tasks executed), *failures* (number of problems, frequency of problems, areas affected by problems, number of repeat problems, number of detected problems, etc.), and *recovery* (problem resolution time).

Phase 5: Control

The control phase gives the manager a means to correct the first four phases on an ongoing basis. In this phase, you can verify whether the measurements meet your objectives. Here, you can reexamine and refine your plans to more effectively support achievement of your objectives, and eliminate execution problems. You can review how you execute your plans, to ensure that the execution has not, itself, caused availability problems. Finally, you can reevaluate your objectives to determine whether they should be upgraded or downgraded, to more effectively balance user requirements against what can actually be achieved.

Phase 5 never ends. Rather, it circles back to Phase 1, giving the manager necessary information for revisiting phases one through four, and creating a closed-loop process. If you skip any of these phases, your management system is likely to become obsolete quickly.

The control phase is crucial to ensuring that the system is consistently managed well. Many IT shops develop excellent plans and objectives, and perform extremely well when they first implement their plans. Since they fail to check on what is happening, however, changing technology, environment, and user requirements leave their management systems behind.

All five phases are interdependent. If you fail to get an accurate picture of user requirements in Phase 1, your plans will be misdirected and insufficient. If you skip planning in favor of early execution, your activities will lead to resource conflicts and poor performance measurements. If managers fail to monitor the process, they cannot determine its ongoing effectiveness.

▶ Identifying the Systems Management Disciplines

If we apply the fundamentals of management to information systems management, we can tabulate the systems management disciplines necessary in any system, big or small. The only difference is how extensively the disciplines are implemented.

Phase	Discipline	Description
1. Setting Objectives	Service-Level Management	Identify, negotiate, and agree to services to be provided, quality measurements, and IT performance targets to be provided to users.
2. Planning	Application & Systems Design	Plan and design IT infrastructure to meet service levels committed to user.
	Capacity Planning	Plan for system growth requirements.
	Configuration Management	Create and maintain system configuration information.
	Asset Management	Create and maintain asset inventory; track and monitor use of such assets.
3. Execution	Problem Management	Detect, record, resolve problems.
	Backup and Recovery	Design alternative systems and resources to immediately restore IT services when problems occur.
4. Measurement	Performance Management	Monitor system performance data; tune system for optimal achievement of service levels committed to users.
5. Control	Change Management	Control all changes to the system to ensure that change does not degrade system performance.
	Security Management	Control and administer access to the system to minimize threats to system integrity.
	Availability Management	Monitor and control system resources and IT operation to maintain system availability.

In our discussion of these systems management disciplines, we do not detail the processes themselves. Rather, we consider the different issues faced when implementing these systems management disciplines. The nitty-gritty of procedures, data, tools, and organization to support these disciplines can differ dramatically for each organization. We therefore focus on the general, common issues encountered by IT organizations, large or small. We also concentrate on the disciplines that are especially critical in today's IT environment, and have the most impact when it comes to addressing users' availability requirements.

Implementing Service-Level Management

▶ Service-Level Management

Service-level management deals with how user service requirements are understood and managed. The objective is to balance what users *want*, and what the business can afford to provide. Begin by examining the business environment and the ways in which information technology supports business objectives. Next, IT negotiates service levels or performance targets with its users. The result of the negotiations is a *service level agreement* — a living document that is revised as the business environment, IT environment, and user requirements change.

Process Requirements

This section describes the process steps involved in service-level management.

Step 1: Define service-level standards

First and foremost, gain a clear understanding of the characteristics users associate with quality service, including system availability, reliability, performance, and usability. In a young IT environment, you can even hold a workshop with users to ensure that you both are "speaking the same language." For example, users may want the system to be fast, but what does 'fast' means to them? Does it mean that the application starts quickly, or that it takes little time to calculate an answer, or that it can quickly fetch data from external databases?

Some common service-level targets deal with the following:

- **Availability hours** — The hours of the day and days of the week that the computer system is accessible to the users.
- **Number of outages** — The average and maximum number of system outages that the users will tolerate. These are two separate targets, and they are equally important. You might have a good average number of outages per day over a given month. For example, you might have experienced only two outages. However, on the day monthly reports were due, you might have had 20 outages.
- **Frequency of outages** — The time between outages. If outages occur in (relatively) rapid succession, more users will be unhappy. Having just recovered from an outage, they will be faced with yet another one.
- **Outage duration** — The length of time an outage can last. Obviously, two outages lasting for one hour each are better than one outage that lasts for more than a day.
- **Response time** — The time it takes for the system to respond to user input.
- **Turnaround time** — The time it takes for a user activity to be completed. This measurement is usually applied to user activities comprising many tasks, such as printing or data retrieval.

Step 2: Establish service levels to be attained

The second step involves the actual negotiations with users on the service levels to be provided. The IT organization should analyze service levels achieved during any pilot implementation programs and determine which of those levels are achievable for all users, what the costs are for reaching those levels, and what action plans can be put in place to achieve levels not previously attained. During negotiations with users, the IT organization should explain the costs of providing the desired service levels, as well as improvements or plans that need to be implemented to make the changes happen. Then, the users can decide whether to invest the resources required to achieve these service levels.

This phase of the service-level negotiation should also identify the people, including representatives from both the IT organization and the user group, who will be responsible for the attainment of the targets set. Remember that service-level management is an ongoing activity, so it is essential that this interaction between the IT group and the users be preserved.

The product of this phase is a Service Level Agreement that is signed by senior management from both the IT organization and the user population. These signatories will guarantee proper focus, attention, and resources are given to enforce the agreement.

Step 3: Monitor achievement of service levels

The next phase in the service-level management discipline concerns measuring whether promised service levels have been achieved.

Since typical service-level targets are defined in high-level terms, first divide these targets into measurable quantities. For example, if you set a target response time of one minute for an employee database system, you may decide to track the time to get back employee data from the moment the Enter key was pressed to the moment data was displayed at the user workstation.

Next, identify and deploy the resources needed to monitor service levels. In the preceding example, this resource could take the form of an IT staffer visiting random user terminals weekly and running a test transaction. Or you might install software on user workstations that automatically executes transactions and records the response time.

Once you deploy resources for monitoring service levels, the third step is to actually monitor them, collecting and storing data for analysis.

Step 4: Analyze service-level attainment and report to higher management

This most crucial and often neglected phase of service-level management involves reporting on service-level attainment. These reports should highlight significant trends, helping to identify problems *before* they become visible to users. Any downtrend in achievement should be spotted and corrected as soon as possible.

Review service-level attainments regularly with user representatives. This offers an excellent opportunity to discuss the challenges you are encountering, and obtain needed support from the users.

Step 5: Redefine service levels, if necessary

Step 5 is the feedback stage of the service-level management process. At this stage, you and your users assess the reasonableness of your service-level targets, and change them if necessary. If the targets cannot be adjusted, then an action plan is devised to help attain them.

Factors that are critical to the success of service-level management are:

- **New targets or service levels piloted** — When you create your first Service Level Agreement, or any new service target, it makes sense to run a pilot program, within IT or with a small group of users, prior to full-scale implementation. This gives you a better understanding of the effort and resources the target will require, including concrete cost data you can use during negotiation with users. A pilot study typically lasts from two to three months.

- **Attainment of service levels monitored** — We see many Service Level Agreements made, then kept under lock and key, never to be reviewed again until a user satisfaction crisis arises. This should *not* happen! IT should use the Service Level Agreement to guide their day-to-day operations, as it defines user expectations in unprecedented detail. IT should also ensure that quantifiable, measurable targets are set. If it can't be measured, don't make it a target.

- **Agreement reevaluated at least once a year** — Reevaluate your Service Level Agreements roughly once a year. This is a comfortable timeframe for the following reasons:

- Major changes in technology and the business environment tend to occur each year.

- If you reevaluate more often, the reevaluations take up too much time, distracting you from actually achieving your targets.

- Your people should be given ample time to achieve their targets.

Data and Measurement Requirements

In this section, we describe the minimum set of data and measurements required for effective service-level management. Then, we list factors critical to the success of data gathering and measurement.

- **System configuration data** — The hardware, software, and other system components installed. The system connection diagram, as well as how the separate components interact with one another. This information is essential for understanding the costs of achieving target service levels.

- **Cost of system operation** — The operational costs of running the system, such as:
  - Staff requirements
  - Recurring costs of hardware, software, and supplies
  - Vendor support requirements (e.g., maintenance contracts)
  - Power, air conditioning, and other environmental costs

- **Service-level measures** — The measurements related to the service-level targets specified in the Service Level Agreement:
  - **Industry benchmarks** — Performance targets accepted in the industry as practical and achievable.
  - **Problem history data** — Information to aid in analysis and reevaluation of the Service Level Agreement.

We recommend the following measures with respect to the performance of service-level management:

- **End-user satisfaction rating** — A measurement derived from periodic surveys asking users how satisfied they are with the service provided by the IT organization.
- **Attainment of service-level targets** — A measurement of how often the IT organization was able to achieve the service-level targets documented in the Service Level Agreement.

Data factors that are critical to the success of service-level management are:

- **Essential service performance measures are available** — We have seen service-level planning sessions become a waste of time because IT did not prepare sufficient system historical performance data. Without this information, users will have no restraints as to what target to ask for, and IT can neither validate nor argue against user requests.
- **Industry performance benchmarks on hand to validate set targets** — IT will naturally set a low target, whereas users will always ask for a high target. Industry benchmarks assist in service-level negotiation process, because they provide objective values that have been achieved elsewhere. Service targets based on industry benchmarks should be more easily acceptable to both IT and users.
- **Users appreciate the costs of desired service levels** — Users always ask for the earth and sky, so you must make them aware that they will pay the cost directly or indirectly. By doing this, you require users to evaluate what they want versus what the business can afford. Treating IT as a business — with its own cost and revenue infrastructure — reinforces the cost issues to users.

Organization Requirements

People responsible for service-level management should have the technical skills to understand the capabilities of the existing computer system as well as alternatives currently available in the market. They should also have data gathering skills to collate measurements related to service levels. During the creation of the service-level document, negotiation skills play a crucial role in its success. Management should choose the right participants in the service-level negotiation activities and give them full authority to decide on behalf of all the other users.

The following organizational factors are critical to the success of service-level management:

- **Support from senior management** — The Service Level Agreement should be a covenant between the highest management of both the IT organization and the users. This ensures that it will be backed with the proper focus, attention, and resource allocation.

- **All users are represented during negotiations** — Because the aim of a Service Level Agreement is to cover all services provided to users, it is but fair that all user groups are represented. If one or two are neglected, sooner or later their complaints will reach high management and you would have to redo your Service Level Agreement. This is because any additional service to be provided to users will impact the IT organization's overall capability of meeting the entire Service Level Agreement.

Tools Requirements

Apart from the typical office productivity tools needed during the creation of the Service Level Agreement, many of the tools required for service-level management measure specific service targets. It is difficult to manually measure from the user's point of view — either users must perform the measurements themselves, or an IT representative must go to the user location, interrupt the user, and perform the measurement. There are few tools to help. Those that are available simulate user keystrokes and record response times. These automated measurement tools must be deployed judiciously, as too many online measurements can degrade system performance.

Tool-related issues critical to the success of service-level management are:

- **Service-level document accessible to all users** — The Service Level Agreement should be read and understood by all members of the IT organization, as it forms the basis for how they will be judged by the users. Users should also have access to this document in case they would like to know more about the system that they use and what to expect (e.g., when the application is available, and how fast it should run.)

- **Measurement of service-level targets done with minimal intervention** — When IT staff find themselves too busy (as is often the case), they set aside monitoring and measuring activities all too often. Worse, if measurements are performed manually, there is greater risk of error, whether accidental or intentional. Accordingly, measurement should be automated whenever possible.

Benefits of Service-Level Management

Many benefits can be realized from a well-implemented service-level management discipline:

- **Harmony between the user and the IT organization** — The most important benefit is that the IT organization gets an accurate picture of what the users need. This may sound trivial, but the lack of well-implemented service-level management disciplines causes most of the rifts between IT and users. A Service Level Agreement is a give-and-take relationship between IT and users. Users articulate what they need, and IT gains support in getting the resources needed to provide it. Both parties must realize that any requested service may be provided, but none come free.
- **Efficiency of IT operations** — Another advantage of having a Service Level Agreement is that IT can allocate just enough resources towards what the users really need. The Service Level Agreement reminds IT of what really matters to the business, so it does not waste resources providing services that are no longer needed, or are too complex and advanced for users. We have seen many IT organizations spend a fortune on technology products that users don't need, simply to create the illusion that IT is on the cutting edge. However, any admiration from users is short-lived if they do not gain any business advantage from those advanced products or services.
- **Improved user satisfaction** — A user of any computing resource will be satisfied if his perceived satisfaction level is exceeded.

With a Service Level Agreement, IT has an opportunity to set this expectation level realistically. IT now has a better chance to satisfy its users, since satisfaction is no longer arbitrary or subjective.

▶ Problem Management

Problem management deals with how problems are handled in the organization. It is a continuous cycle process that encompasses problem detection, documentation of the problem and its resolution, identification and testing of the solution, resolution, closing the problem, and generating statistical reports.

Process Requirements

This section describes key process steps for managing problems.

Step 1: Define problem management process and practices

The first step in establishing an effective problem management discipline is to publish a plan on how to handle problems. This plan should cover:

- **Procedures for handling problems** — What is done after a problem is detected and reported, how problem data is captured and stored, and how the problem is managed to resolution.
- **Roles and responsibilities of the IT support staff** — Who receives the problem, who records all information, who handles problem resolution, and what each entity is supposed to do.
- **Measurements for problem resolution** — What will be tracked to monitor the efficiency of the problem management discipline.
- **Tools to be used** — See below.
- **Problems to be handled and how to classify them** — Severity and priority assignment methodology, as well as escalation guidelines.

- **Bypass procedures** — Actions that can be taken to immediately restore system availability in the event of certain specific events or problems.

Step 2: Detect or recognize the problem

In this step, activate the necessary tools to detect problems. Use all facilities for capturing problem reports, including the help desk. Gather data, and record all pertinent information in a location accessible to all support staffers. Notify affected users to help them minimize the impact of the problem.

Step 3: Bypass the problem

As soon as the problem is detected, take all possible steps to bypass it or minimize its impact on users. Ideally, identify bypass procedures in advance, ensuring that they have no side effect on other systems, applications, or users. Recognize that a bypass is *not* a resolution of the problem. All too often, problem bypasses are left installed and treated as a permanent fix, only to have the system eventually fail because the bypass was not designed to run forever, or because the bypass impacted other systems.

In some cases, bypass procedures are invoked so often that they become the norm for "solving" the problem, when they do little to prevent the problem from happening again. Some simple examples of bypasses that don't represent permanent solutions are:

- Rebooting a server or network router without identifying the source of the failure.
- Pressing "CTRL-ALT-DELETE" when the PC hangs instead of finding the failing software application and fixing it.
- Choosing Retry or Ignore when presented with a "Diskette write error, Abort Retry Ignore." Sooner or later, the user will find his data completely unrecoverable because he chose not to reformat or replace his diskette.

Record all bypass activities along with the problem information so that when the problem is passed to other support staffers, no relevant information is lost.

Step 4: Analyze the problem

At this stage, identify the true cause of the problem, and evaluate, test, and apply possible resolutions. Review historical records of related problems to see if similar problems are on record. Efficient, effective problem analysis can significantly reduce the time it takes for resolution.

Step 5: Manage the problem to resolution

Often, a single support professional cannot resolve a problem entirely on his own. Problems must be shared amongst multiple support staffers, especially if they are complex or involve multiple systems or applications. In these cases, it is important that there is an entity to monitor and manage the problem to resolution, ensuring that it is resolved within the process performance targets.

Management of problems also involves escalation to higher management and support staffers when the problem is repetitive or has occurred before, has not been resolved during the set resolution times, affects many users, or has a serious impact on the business.

Once the problem has been fixed, flag it as *temporarily* closed for a given period of time, such as one week. After this period lapses, ask the affected users if the problem has recurred, or if any unwanted effects were caused by the fix. If not, you can close the problem permanently.

Step 6: Report on the status and trends of problems

Gather problem statistics and generate summary reports to aid in identifying trends and implementing preventive measures. These reports may include:

- **Summary of closed problems** — Problems that occurred, how long it took to resolve them, and what the solutions were
- **Status of open problems** — Existing unresolved problems, when they were opened, and why they remain as unresolved action items
- **Problem trends and statistics** — Number and type of problems, areas affected, frequency of occurrence

- **Root cause of problems report** — Problems that occurred, why they occurred, what can be done to prevent recurrence

- **Action plan for the next period** — Plans to improve on problem trends and resolution times

These reports inform IT management of the current health of the system *and* offer a way to communicate with users on IT's support activities.

Step 7: Redefine the problem management process if necessary

Sometimes, delays in resolving problems are not due to the complexity of the problems, but to a failure of managing the problems to resolution. This step provides a way to refine or enhance the existing management discipline, based on the measurements that have been achieved. It is part of the continuing improvement cycle of this and all other systems management disciplines.

The following process factors are critical to the success of problem management:

- **All problems, big and small, are covered** — Small problems lead to (or are symptoms of) bigger problems, so it is important that *all* problems are recorded. The recurring data read error eventually becomes a bad diskette problem. The intermittent LAN connection problem sooner or later turns out to be a broken cabling problem. And the nuisance "General Protection Fault" error in Windows is likely due to a bad memory component.

- **Escalation procedures are followed** — Many IT support staffers mistakenly believe that escalating a problem is an admission of incompetence, so they violate established escalation guidelines. This situation is dangerous — IT management loses control over the problem, often without even realizing it.

- **Problems are assigned severity levels and prioritized accordingly** — We've said that all problems should be covered, but we did not say that all should be treated the same. On the contrary, you need a severity and priority assignment methodology that ensures important problems are handled first. A problem may be deemed as more severe if one or more of the following conditions are true:

- Multiple users are affected
- Critical business function cannot be performed
- Alternate systems are not available
- Entire system is not available

- **Users are updated on the status of the problems** — Users experience major frustration when they have to wait for IT support staff to update them on the status of a problem. It is thus imperative that the IT staffer in charge of managing the problem regularly updates affected users as often as possible. Users appreciate knowing what has been done, the current status of the problem, and when to expect a resolution.

- **Problem trends are analyzed and measures are taken to address them** — The objective of systems management is to make everyone proactive in resolving problems. Wherever possible, you should prevent problems from occurring, instead of simply resolving them after they are already causing business losses. The analysis of problem statistics is a valuable tool for achieving this goal, because it helps identify potential problems based on past experience.

Data Requirements

For an effective problem management discipline, the following information is necessary:

- **Problem information**
  - Date and time that the problem occurred
  - Circumstances prior to problem occurrence
  - Symptoms of the problem
  - Affected systems or applications
  - Impact on the users
- **System configuration data**
  - Hardware and software inventory
  - Configuration diagram
  - Network diagram
  - Cabling diagram

- **Escalation information**
  - Support assignments and skills matrix
  - Vendor agreements and contracts
  - Service Level Agreements
  - Availability requirements
  - Outage duration and frequency limits
- **Resolution information**
  - Actions done
  - By whom
  - Results
  - Action plans
  - Ultimate resolution

The following measurements are recommended:

- **Number of problems**
  - By severity
  - By affected area
  - By period (daily, weekly, or monthly)
- **Problem resolution time** — The time needed to resolve the problem from the time the call was first placed. Some organizations only count the number of business hours, others count based on a 24-hour per day period. We suggest basing the count on the hours of committed system availability. If you have committed to provide 24 hour a day, 7 days a week availability, measure in terms of continuous hours. This approach provides a fair and accurate picture of the help desk's efficiency in resolving calls.
- **Number of repeat calls** — The number of calls that represent recurrences of previously closed calls. Set a time limit to use as a basis for defining a call as a repeat call — typically one to two weeks. Your objective is to measure the quality of the help desk's fixes. More repeat calls indicate poorer problem determination and resolution skills.

Data factors that are critical to the success of problem management are:

- **All problems are recorded** — As emphasized above, insignificant problems often lead to major problems. If they are not recorded and monitored, they may cause future outages. Unfortunately, repetitive minor problems are tedious to record manually, so the help desk or individual assigned to record them may fail to log all occurrences. The solution is to automate problem detection and logging, implementing tools that monitor system status and automatically generate problem reports or tickets when necessary.
- **All information pertaining to the problem is available to the problem handler** — All too often, key information about problems and attempts to resolve them is lost when problems are passed between support staffers. This can result in repetition of past activities, and ultimately a prolonged resolution time. All activities, their results, and action plans must be logged and provided to whoever handles a problem next.

Organization Requirements

We have yet to see a problem management discipline work effectively without a help desk to serve as a central location for reporting and managing problems. The help desk serves as the interface between the users and the IT organization, offering many advantages to both IT and users:

- Users have a single entity to contact for any problem — they are not required to identify and track down the right IT staff member. This eliminates both wasted time and frustration.
- The help desk filters calls for IT support, so minor calls no longer trouble IT professionals with more urgent priorities.
- The help desk manages the problem to resolution, ensuring that others within the IT organization take required actions within appropriate timeframes.

Help desk staffers need both technical and support skills. The help desk *as a whole* should have the necessary technical skills to support the entire breadth of installed hardware and software. If your support staff does not yet possess these skills, contract with third-party service providers to step in when a problem cannot be resolved in-house.

Establish an escalation path for unresolved problems, especially for those with high severity or priority. This escalation path should cover all possible major system outages.

The following organization factors are critical to the success of problem management:

- **Owners are assigned to problems** — As managers quickly realize, "If a problem has many owners, it has no real owner." *Someone* must be ultimately responsible for a problem's resolution — even if his role is just to manage the resources or people needed to solve the problem. For most problems, the help desk can take this responsibility.

- **An escalation path exists for unresolved problems** — Clear escalation paths for unresolved problems are utterly crucial. We have seen some IT organizations with gaps in their support structure for critical system components such as LAN infrastructure or server hardware. Ideally, your escalation paths should lead all the way to the designer or manufacturer of the critical system component. This is why we advocate establishing vendor support agreements. These may be formal maintenance contracts, or simply commitments of priority assistance in the event of a severe problem.

Tools Requirements

For an effective help desk, you need facilities or tools to receive calls, handle and resolve problems, and create reports. Here are the *minimum* tools required:

- **For receiving calls and handling the problem, you need:**
  - A room or location for the help desk staffers
  - A table, an incoming telephone line (for receiving user calls), and an outgoing telephone line (for interacting with the users after the initial call)
  - A call logging facility (e.g., spreadsheet, database program, browser-based intranet application, or shrinkwrapped help desk software)

- Space for storing call records, printed manuals, and other resources

- **For resolving the call and creating reports, you need:**
    - A computer system configured to match typical end-user equipment
    - Word processing and charting software
    - A printer
    - Manuals and references
    - Access to system resources as needed (e.g., server administration)

Tools or equipment factors critical to the success of problem management are:

- **Automatic detection of problems** — Ideally, the help desk or IT organization should often detect problems before users do. Early detection not only improves user satisfaction, it also reduces outage duration, since steps to resolve the problem can be taken sooner. This automation is most common in network monitoring where network resources can be polled for availability, and if the resources cannot be reached, the monitor can generate an alert automatically. Similarly, automated antivirus software can immediately detect the presence of viruses before the infection spreads to other files, computers, or systems.

- **Logging facility for all problems, with the ability to generate summary reports** — The greater the quantity and frequency of problems to be managed, the greater the need for computerization of logging, tracking, and reporting. Help desks that try to make do with manual monitoring and logbooks miss many important problems, or must use far more staff to keep up with the workload. The logging facility can be as simple as a spreadsheet program if the volume of problems is low. However, consider the benefits of help desk management software that provides automatic problem ticket generation, access from remote workstations, automatic report generation, and other advantages.

Benefits of Problem Management

Numerous benefits can be realized from a well-implemented project management discipline:

- **Solve repetitive problems** — Most repetitive problems recur simply because the right solution is not identified, or the same unsuccessful solutions are tried repeatedly by different support staff handling the same type of problem. This situation arises not because the technical support staffers are incapable of finding the right solution, but because no accurate, detailed records have been kept on what has been tried before. A well-implemented problem management discipline prevents repetitive problems from occurring.

- **Reduce number and impact of problems** — Many of the problems encountered by IT organizations have happened before, so if problem management is done correctly, the root causes of such problems can be identified, and appropriate solutions applied, preventing the problem from recurring.

- **Reduce problem resolution time** — An effective problem management discipline "remembers" past solutions to problems, so when those problems occur again elsewhere, the stored knowledge can be used to accelerate resolution, often eliminating the need for problem isolation, identification, and analysis.

- **Improve support staff productivity** — More than 70 percent of a typical IT worker's time is spent fixing problems instead of designing and deploying new applications or systems. This crisis mode of operation can be traced directly to ineffective problem management systems.

▶ Change Management

Change management deals with how changes to the system are managed so they do not degrade system performance and availability. Many people mistakenly view change management as more IT red tape. They fail to realize that good change management acts like a traffic light that regulates the smooth flow of changes, and does *not* stop all change from happening. The objective of change management is to ensure that changes do not negatively impact system performance as a whole.

Change management means that all changes should be identified and planned for prior to implementation. Backout procedures should be established in case changes create problems. Then, after changes are applied, they are thoroughly tested and evaluated.

Change management is especially critical in today's highly decentralized, client-centric environment, where users themselves may be applying many changes. A key cause of high TCO is the application of changes by those who do not fully understand their implications across the operating environment.

Process Requirements

This section describes the process steps for change management and discusses factors critical to the success of change management.

Step 1: Define change management process and practices

As with other systems management disciplines, first craft a plan for handling changes. This plan should cover:

- **Procedures for handling changes** — How changes are requested, how they are processed and scheduled for implementation, how they are applied, and what the criteria are for backing out changes that cause problems.

- **Roles and responsibilities of the IT support staff** — Who receives the change request, who tracks all change requests, who schedules change implementations, and what each entity is supposed to do.

- **Measurements for change management** — What will be tracked to monitor the efficiency of the change management discipline.

- **Tools to be used** — See below.

- **Type of changes to be handled and how to assign priorities** — Priority assignment methodology and escalation guidelines.

- **Backout procedures** — Actions to take if applied changes do not perform as expected or cause problems to other components of the system.

Step 2: Receive change requests

Receive all requests for changes, ideally through a single change coordinator. Change requests can be submitted on a change request form that includes the date and time of the request.

Step 3: Plan for implementation of changes

Examine all change requests to determine:

- Change request prioritization
- Resource requirements for implementing the change
- Impact to the system
- Backout procedures
- Schedule of implementation

Step 4: Implement and monitor the changes, back out changes if necessary

At this stage, apply the change and monitor the results. If the desired outcome is not achieved, or if other systems or applications are negatively affected, back out the changes.

Step 5: Evaluate and report on changes implemented

Provide feedback on all changes to the change coordinator, whether they were successful or not. The change coordinator is responsible for examining trends in the application of changes, to see if:

- Change implementation planning was sufficient
- Changes to certain resources are more prone to problems

When a change has been successfully made, it is crucial that the corresponding system information store be updated to reflect them.

Step 6: Modify change management plan if necessary

You may need to modify the entire change management process to make it more effective. Consider reexamining your change management discipline if:

- Changes are not being applied on time
- Not enough changes are being processed
- Too many changes are being backed out
- Changes are affecting the system availability
- Not all changes are being covered

Process-related issues critical to the success of change management are:

- **Changes are evaluated and tested prior to implementation** — It is practically impossible to predict the outcome of all changes especially in a complex, interrelated system architecture. Hence, a thorough evaluation of all changes must be carried out, especially those dealing with critical system resources. We also highly recommend that all changes be tested prior to full-scale deployment. For minimum impact on the system, test with a user not on the critical path, with test data, during off hours, on a test system.
- **All changes, big and small, are covered** — Minor changes can have major effects on system performance and availability. A simple change in a shared database's file name could cause all applications that use it to fail. An additional software utility installed in the user's workstation could cause his system to become unstable. Or a move of a user's workstation from one department to another could prevent it from properly accessing the network. You might occasionally need to bypass certain change management processes, as for emergency changes required to recover from a fault condition. But even in these cases, document the change thoroughly, and have it approved after implementation, to ensure that system records are updated.
- **All changes are documented** — Perhaps the hardest part of change management is documenting all actions performed before, during, and after the change has been applied. Technical people often fail to document changes, and we have seen many problems caused because not everyone knew about earlier

changes. Many IT organizations are familiar with the Monday Morning Crisis — wherein most problems occur on Monday mornings because someone implemented a change over the weekend without following correct change management procedures.

Data Requirements

All change requests should contain the following information:

- Name of requestor
- Function or position of requestor
- Date and time of request
- Desired date for implementation of change
- Change request description
- Reason for change
- Procedures for backing out change if necessary
- User management approval

All system documentation should be current and available. If it is not, you have virtually no chance of being able to plan and implement changes successfully. You must have *at least* the following system information available:

- **Physical resource map** or location diagram
- **Cabling diagram,** including from/to connections and cable labels
- **Network diagram,** including component names and addresses
- **Application and data hierarchical diagram,** covering the critical software components and applications

The following information should be monitored to evaluate the success of your change management discipline:

- **Change turnaround time** — From the time of request to the time that the change has been successfully implemented
- **Number of changes implemented**

- **Number and severity of problems** due to changes
- **Number of changes backed out** — Changes that were implemented but had to be removed due to problems

Data requirement factors that are critical to the success of change management are:

- **All components affected by a change are identified** — You need to understand the physical, data, network, and computational dependencies among system components. This is only possible if system configuration data is complete and updated.
- **All changes are immediately reflected in system documentation** — As soon as the change is implemented and deemed successful, the system documentation should be updated. This practice prevents errors on the part of other IT staff members when dealing with that changed resource. It also supports the asset and configuration management discipline, as discussed below.

Organization Requirements

It is essential that there be a single entity that receives, approves, and monitors all changes. As we have said before, changes usually impact other resources because of today's interconnected IT environment. Without this centralized processing, changes *will* get out of hand. TCO studies have repeatedly found that users' ability to change workstation configurations arbitrarily is a key cause of additional support costs.

The central change management entity should be given management support in dealing with users who do not abide by the change management guidelines. It should also include people with skill in assessing all change requests, even if only to identify affected resources and in-house expertise.

All change requests should be approved prior to implementation. No changes should be implemented without a signoff from the change management body. Even emergency changes should be approved, to preclude the practice of bypassing the change management process with spurious emergency changes.

A possible exception to the approval rule is ongoing operational changes. In these cases, system operators can be given blanket approval to implement such changes, provided that (a) the changes appear on a list of preapproved changes and (b) all changes are written in a change log that is regularly reviewed and signed by the system operator's immediate manager.

Tools Requirements

A facility for receiving and recording all change requests should be available. Depending on the number of changes to be managed, this facility could be automated by means of specialized change management software.

The use of change monitoring software is also recommended in client-server environments where changes in PC and server configuration are difficult to control. This type of software can take a snapshot of a systems configuration, and then regularly compare the existing configuration versus what it has on record. If a discrepancy is found, an alarm can be triggered, allowing the IT organization to take action. An additional benefit derived from this tool is the availability of backup configuration data necessary to recover a corrupted system.

Because no amount of planning can completely predict the outcome of changes to complex systems, a test system should be made available for trying out changes before they are implemented on a production or online system. The need for this test system would depend on the criticality of the system resource or change. These test systems can also serve as backup resources if a primary resource encounters a severe outage.

Benefits

Among the benefits to be realized from effective change management are:

- **Fewer problems due to changes** — Many problems can be prevented if changes are controlled. Call statistics from help desks in major IT organizations agree — the users themselves introduce many problems. User-introduced problems are usually due to the unauthorized installation of software, modification of system configuration parameters, and deletion of critical system files. IT organizations have begun to lose faith in users' ability to discipline themselves when it comes to changes, and are removing the users' ability to introduce these changes. For example, some IT organizations remove diskette drives, disable write capability on local storage, prevent access to the inside of computers, and take other precautions.

- **Better control over system configuration integrity** — If you can monitor and control all changes, you can more easily maintain the integrity of your system configuration. Changes to system hardware or software configuration, intentionally or accidentally, might otherwise easily go unnoticed for long periods of time. We have seen pilferage of computer memory from user workstations that organizations had no way to detect or prevent, because their PCs had no physical security features. When it came time to install a new application, the system would not perform adequately because the hardware configuration had been tampered with. And, of course, there are recurring computer virus incidents due to users installing the latest shareware downloadable from the Internet.

▶ Security Management

Security management deals with how system integrity is maintained amid possible man-made threats and risks, intentional or unintentional. Intentional man-made threats include espionage, hacks, computer viruses, etc. Unintentional threats include those due to accidents or user ignorance of the effects of their actions.

Security management ranges from identification of risks to determination of security measures and controls, detection of violations, and analysis of security violations.

Process Requirements

This section describes the process steps involved in security management, and discusses factors critical to the success of security management.

Step 1: Determine and evaluate of IT assets

Three types of assets must be identified:

- **Physical** — Computer hardware and software resources, building facilities, and resources used to house sensitive assets or process sensitive information.
- **Information** — Sensitive data pertaining to the company's operations, plans, and strategies. Examples are marketing and sales plans, detailed financial data, trade secrets, personnel information, IT infrastructure data, user profiles and passwords, sensitive office correspondence, minutes of meetings, etc. Lately, there is also concern about protecting company logos and materials posted on the public Internet.
- **People** — Vital individuals holding key roles, whose incapacity or absence will impact the business in one way or another.

After you identify company assets, the next step is to determine their security level. Depending on the company's requirements, assets may be classified into two, three, or more levels of security, depending on the value of the asset being protected. We recommend having only two levels for organizations with minimal security threats: public and confidential. A three-level security classification scheme can be implemented if security needs are greater: public, confidential, and restricted.

Be wary of having too many security levels, as this tends to dilute their importance in the eyes of the user. A large multinational IT vendor used to have four levels of security: public, internal use only, confidential, confidential restricted, and registered confidential. Today, they have cut it down to three: *public, internal use only,* and *confidential.* Employees were getting confused as to the differences between the secured levels, and the procedures associated with each one. Having too many security levels proved expensive in terms of employee education, security facilities, and office practices — the costs were often greater than the potential losses from a security violation.

Step 2: Analyze risk

Every effective security management system reflects a careful evaluation of how much security is needed. Too little security means the system can easily be compromised intentionally or unintentionally. Too much security can make the system hard to use or degrade its performance unacceptably. Security is inversely proportional to utility — if you want the system to be 100 percent secure, don't let anybody use it. There will always be risks to systems, but often these risks are accepted if they make the system more powerful or easier to use.

Sources of risks to assets can be *intentional* (criminals, hackers, or terrorists; competitors; disgruntled employees; or self-serving employees) or *unintentional* (careless employees; poorly trained users and system operators; vendors and suppliers).

Acceptance of risk is central to good security management. You will never have enough resources to secure assets 100 percent; in fact, this is virtually impossible even with unlimited resources. Therefore, identify all risks to the system, then choose which risks to accept and which to address via security measures. Here are a few reasons why some risks are acceptable:

- The threat is minimal
- The possibility of compromise is unlikely
- The value of the asset is low
- The cost to secure the asset is greater than the value of the asset
- The threat will soon go away
- Security violations can easily be detected and immediately corrected

After the risks are identified, the next step is to determine the impact to the business if the asset is lost or compromised. By doing this, you get a good idea of how many resources should be assigned to protecting the asset. One user workstation almost certainly deserves fewer resources than the company's servers.

The risks you choose to accept should be documented and signed by all parties, not only to protect the IT organization, but also to make everybody aware that unsecured company assets do exist.

Step 3: Define security practices

Define in detail the following key areas of security management:

- **Asset classification practices** — Guidelines for specifying security levels as discussed above.
- **Risk assessment and acceptance** — As above.
- **Asset ownership** — Assignment of roles for handling sensitive assets.
- **Asset handling responsibilities** — The different tasks and procedures to be followed by the different entities handling the asset, as identified above.
- **Policies** — Regarding mishandling of security assets
- **How security violations are reported** and responded to
- **Security awareness practices** — Education programs, labeling of assets.
- **Security audits** — Unannounced checks of security measures put in place to find out whether they are functioning.

Step 4: Implement security practices

At this phase, implement the security measures defined in the preceding step. You can do this in stages to make it easier for everybody to adapt to the new working environment. Expect many problems at the start, especially with respect to user resistance to their security tasks, such as using passwords. Staged implementation can be performed:

- **By department,** starting with the most sensitive assets. The natural first choice would be the IT department.
- **By business function or activity,** starting with those that depend upon (or create) the most sensitive assets. You might begin with all Business Planning activities, followed by Marketing, Human Resources, etc.
- **By location,** especially if prioritized sensitive assets are mostly physical. This approach is easiest to implement. However, its effectiveness is doubtful for information assets residing in networked computer systems. You might start with the IT data center, then gradually widen the secured area to encompass the entire business facility.
- **By people,** starting with key members of the organization.

Step 5: Monitor for violations and take corresponding actions

An effective security management discipline depends on adequate compliance monitoring. Violations of security practices, whether intentional or unintentional, become more frequent and serious if not detected and acted upon. A computer hacker who gets away with the first system penetration will return repeatedly if he knows no one can detect his activities. Users who get away with leaving confidential documents on their desks will get into bad habits if not corrected quickly.

There are two major activities here: *detecting* security violations and *responding* to them. With respect to sensitive assets, it is important to know:

- Who has the right to handle the assets (user names)
- How to authenticate those asset users (password, IDs, etc.)
- Who has tried to gain access to them
- How to restrict access to allowed activities
- Who has tried to perform actions beyond those that are allowed

Document the response to security violations, and follow up immediately after a violation is detected. The IT organization should have a Computer Emergency Response Team to deal with security violations. Members of this team should have access to senior management so that severe situations can easily be escalated.

Responses can be built into your security tools or facilities to ensure that the response to a violation is immediate. For example, a password checking utility may be designed to lock out a user name immediately after three invalid password entries. Alarms can be installed around the data center facility so that if any window or door is forced open, security guards or police are immediately notified.

A critical part of this activity is the generation of reports for management that discuss significant security violations and trends of minor incidences. The objective is to spot potential major security violations before they cause serious damage.

Step 6: Reevaluate IT assets and risks

Security management is a discipline that never rests. Some major changes that would require a reassessment of the security management practice are:

- Security violations are rampant
- Organizational structure or composition changes
- Business environment changes
- Technology changes
- Budget allocation decreases

The following process factors are critical to the success of security management:

- **All incidents of security violations are recorded** — Almost all major security problems begin as minor incidents that are left unchecked. A new virus incident starts in a single workstation and quickly spreads to neighboring computers if not immediately detected and acted upon. A hacker attempting to break into a secured server begins by trying to log on using different IDs and password combinations, eventually succeeding if the system administrator does not act. These and other examples highlight the need to capture and record every security-related incident no matter how trivial it seems.

- **Summary and trend reports are analyzed for potential major security breaches in the future** — Recording security violations is pointless unless you also review summary and trend reports pertaining to security. For example, reports on the nature and number of security violations by user or department will help identify individuals posing a security threat, intentional or otherwise.

Data Requirements

Information is key to any effective security management discipline. This information at times may be hard to come by if no tools are available to automate data collection. This data helps not only in planning but also in implementation and evaluation. The data required by this discipline includes four categories:

- **Assets** — Draw up a list of corporate assets, describe the location of secured assets, and list the assets' owners. Next, prioritize the security level for the assets, and identify the weaknesses and vulnerabilities of each asset.
- **Users** — Keep a current list of users of secured assets, their user IDs and passwords. Determine how to control activities by defining:
  - Allowable activities, by asset and type of user
  - User access times
  - System configuration data
  - Security features of existing system resources
- **Incidents** — Record invalid access attempts by source, time, and resource accessed. Establish a response protocol that includes:
  - Emergency response team members and contact information
  - Security incident reporting and response policies and guidelines
- **Measurements** — To track effectiveness of the implementation of the security management disciplines, track the following:
  - Number of outages due to security violations
  - Time to detect a security violation
  - Time to eliminate security threat

Data-related factors critical to the success of security management are:

- **Sensitive assets are identified** — Obviously, one must know what one has to protect. In a corporate environment, this knowledge comes from those who own or use the asset and is communicated to those responsible for securing the IT environment. *Your system is only as strong as its weakest link.* It follows that the identification of sensitive assets should be as thorough as possible. For example, where are confidential marketing plans stored (which servers, user workstations, storage devices, user desks) and in what forms (data file, hard copy format)?
- **Security policies are documented and well publicized** — In a distributed computing environment, systems management roles and

responsibilities are also distributed to the remote departments and their users. It is thus vital that everybody in the organization is aware of corporate security practices, so they can ensure their own compliance and that of their colleagues. This helps deputize everybody in the enforcement of security practices, enhancing the reach and effectiveness of the security organization. Take, for example, the policy of wearing IDs inside office premises to help identify valid employees and guests versus those without authorization to be there — a simple but effective first step in securing the office environment. If everybody is aware of this policy, they can help in its enforcement by challenging anyone they see without proper identification. Some offices use visitor IDs with their destination clearly marked (e.g., second floor) so that if a visitor is seen in other locations, employees are easily alerted.

- **All possible threats are identified and understood** — Know what you are up against. Know what hackers can exploit to get into your system. Keep yourself updated on the latest hacking techniques and practices, as well as the most recently discovered vulnerabilities of your system, by joining mailing lists of public IT security organizations such as CERT, by getting bug-related alerts for your critical system components, and possibly even by joining hacker organizations to hear what they're talking about.

Some popular (and effective) means by which hackers can break into systems include:

- **Dumpster diving** — Going through office garbage in search of sensitive data such as employee lists, personnel information, user IDs, schedules, and access numbers. Hackers use this information to enter the corporate facility by pretending to be someone else. The objective of the hacker is to get user IDs and passwords to gain system access, or get telephone numbers of modems for remote access.
- **War dialing** — The entry of user account names and passwords until a match is found. Once a hacker has access to user IDs, he can easily use war dialing in combination with different passwords to gain access to online systems. Statistics have shown this to be an effective hacking technique because users lack awareness of password security. All too often, they leave default

passwords unchanged, use their user name as a password, leave passwords in place for months, or use the names of pets, family members, or famous personalities. In fact, hackers circulate a list of common user passwords that have high success rates. If this approach fails, hackers can simply employ programs that try out every possible password until a match is found.

- **Use of sniffers and other network listening devices** — Sophisticated hackers can use devices that tap into network traffic and decode the data that passes. With this approach, the user is unaware that all his communications have been compromised. Tapping into the network is usually done physically when the hacker has access to the network cables. It is also possible to tap into network traffic between remote routers and servers.

Organization Requirements

Information security in today's environment entails carefully distributing roles and responsibilities throughout the organization. This top-down approach is necessary because sensitive assets are also scattered throughout the enterprise. Securing of assets can be distributed as follows:

- **Asset owners** — The entity that creates the asset. For example, personnel databases are owned by the Human Resources department, marketing strategies are owned by the marketing department or by the sales manager that created it, and user IDs and passwords are owned by the IT security administrator and individual users. The asset owner does the following:
  - Determines the value of the asset and classifies its security requirement accordingly
  - Periodically checks on the security controls in place for that particular asset
  - Authorizes who may gain access
  - Participates in risk assessment and risk acceptance
  - Brings security exposures and violations to management attention

- **Users** — The person who uses the asset. The user does the following:
  - Complies with the security requirements of the asset
  - Uses the assets for approved purposes only
  - Brings security exposures and violations to management attention
- **Managers** — The person who manages or has responsibility for the users of the asset. A manager does the following:
  - Manages assets assigned to them
  - Authorizes the use of resources where assets reside
  - Educates users on security practices
  - Responds to security exposures and violations
  - Performs security self-assessments on a regular basis
- **IT operations** — The entity that operates the systems and resources on which the assets reside. IT operations does the following:
  - Administers security mechanisms and tools
  - Detects and responds to security exposures and violations
  - Brings security exposures and violations to management attention

Organizational factors that are critical to the success of security management are:

- **Support from the highest management of the company** — Security policies should be implemented from the top of the organization down through all the levels of the organization. Top management should make the observance of security practices a condition for employment. Without this kind of management support, any security management practice is bound to fail since users will not give it the attention and respect it deserves.
- **Distribution of security responsibilities across the organization** — The assignment of responsibilities to asset owners, users, management, and IT operations is crucial in today's highly distributed computing environment. As more of IT's resources fall into the hands of users, it becomes even more difficult for the IT organization to monitor and control access to sensitive assets located in those resources. Hence, the only way for security management to succeed is if the users themselves practice safe computing.

- **Establishment of an emergency response team** — In a crisis, it will be difficult to get everybody in the security chain to work together quickly. As a stopgap solution, an emergency response team can be created and given the support and authority to act on behalf of asset owners and management during major security incidents. Such incidents can include:
  - Major system outages (e.g., natural calamities)
  - Computer virus incidents, which always have the potential of spreading throughout the organization
  - Break-ins to sensitive resources (e.g., penetration of network firewall)

The emergency response team is typically composed of a representative from the user population, someone from management, and the best people from the IT organization. They should be on call at all times, and well trained to handle all types of security emergencies.

Tools Requirements

Tools are more and more necessary as the number of systems to be monitored and the amount of traffic and usage data to examine increases. In security management, tools are usually employed to:

- Monitor user logins and logouts
- Record invalid login attempts
- Automatically respond to invalid login attempts based on pre-defined limits set by the security administrator (e.g., invalidate a user ID after three invalid password inputs)
- Administer user IDs and passwords, including password management facilities (e.g., restrict passwords to certain lengths, disallow common words as passwords, automatically expire passwords after a set amount of time.)
- Record user activities (e.g., monitoring cameras in secured office areas)
- Render data unreadable by unauthorized parties, using encryption algorithms
- Establish a perimeter of defense between trusted and untrusted systems through the use of a firewall

Tool-related factors that are critical to the success of security management are:

- **Tools are current and updated to guard against the latest security problems** — Having the wrong security tool can be worse than having no security tool at all. Having a tool gives the IT organization and the business a sense of security that may be unwarranted if the tool is outdated. For example, some organizations rely on outdated antivirus software, letting their guard down when it comes to limiting the use of software from outside sources, since they believe they are protected. As a consequence, newer computer viruses are able to penetrate the system and introduce problems.

  If a security tool is used, it should always be reevaluated regularly to see if it is still effective in preventing security-related problems. For example, in the future, consider migrating to encryption software with longer key lengths, since technological advances will eventually render today's key lengths easily breakable by brute force "guessing" algorithms.

- **Users are aware of the limitations of security tools** — Information security is a continuing battle between those who protect and those who violate, so you should realize that no security tool is without its limitations. It is incumbent upon the security administrator to make users aware of the limitations of their security systems (but not necessarily telling them how to violate their security systems). For example, antivirus software will always be playing catch-up with the latest computer viruses, so users should continue to practice safe installation and avoid the use of software from unverified public sources such as the Internet. Password protection systems are another example — they will fail if a user writes down his password in an easily accessible location.

Benefits

There are numerous benefits to be realized from an effective security management discipline.

- **Reduce problems due to external factors, man-made or other-wise** — Many problems can be avoided if risks are adequately identified and acted on before they impact system availability. We have seen many network outages from people accidentally tripping over network cables — something which could easily have been prevented if that possibility had been foreseen and forestalled by running cables under raised flooring or even by fastening them to the floor with tape.
- **Secure company assets** — Good security practices ensure that company assets are used to their fullest, since assets are protected from damage or loss, whether temporary or permanent.

▶ Asset and Configuration Management

Asset and configuration management are two closely related systems management disciplines. We discuss them together because one without the other will not work. Asset management tackles the need to control the use of company assets, while configuration management deals with how these assets are configured or organized across the organization. Taken together, the objective of these disciplines is to ensure that corporate asset information is thorough and accurate. These disciplines encompass several tasks: asset inventories, documentation of system configuration, documentation of changes to system configuration, and reporting on the status of all assets.

Process Requirements

This section describes the process of asset and configuration management, and discusses factors critical to the success of asset and configuration management.

Step 1: Define asset and configuration data requirements

First understand what types of asset and configuration information are required by the other systems management disciplines. Asset and configuration management is a supporting discipline that only functions for the sake of the other disciplines. For example, security management needs an accurate list of systems connected to the corporate server to effectively administer user access permissions — information that can only be provided by this discipline. (See the section on data requirements later in this chapter.)

Step 2: Identify asset and configuration information gathering and update procedures

This step examines the information requirements identified in step 1 and identifies the best ways to obtain these information elements and maintain their currency.

Automated tools can regularly interrogate systems for information such as processor type, memory size, and other hardware components. Newer PCs make this information easily available by incorporating system configuration data maintenance facilities into their BIOS. Also important is user workstation software configuration for critical software installed, especially with respect to the operating system.

In some cases, the only way to get configuration information is by on-site inspection. Such is the case with older equipment, which uses internal switches to set key configuration information. Cable configuration data presents an especially great challenge to many IT organizations.

Step 3: Gather asset and configuration information and update procedures

At this stage, collect asset information and quickly incorporate it into existing data stores to ensure that the data remains current. The schedule of getting updated asset and configuration information depends on the following factors:

- **The number of changes occurring in the system** — The greater the number, the more often configuration information should be checked and updated.
- **The criticality of changes in the system** — For changes that impact many different system components, information regarding the new asset or its configuration needs to be as current as possible.
- **The urgency of getting updated information** — Urgency is dictated by the other systems management disciplines. Sometimes,

an urgent requirement comes about because of a system activity that must be performed quickly, and requires up-to-date information.

For example, a database server goes down and its data must be restored to another server. Restoration requires access to the list of applications residing on that server, along with the most current list of users requiring access to those applications. User workstations would then have to be reconfigured to access the alternate server (unless this was already set to switch over to the alternate server automatically).

Step 4: Provide information to other systems management disciplines

Make asset and configuration information easily accessible to members of the IT organization performing other systems management functions. Ideally, every time an asset or configuration changes, all systems management owners should be alerted, especially for major changes. This notification can be done via intranet, email, office memos, or other electronic means.

As you can see, change management plays a crucial role in ensuring that the asset and configuration information is current. If changes do not go through the predefined procedures for change implementation, including updates to system configuration information, asset and configuration management cannot function effectively.

Step 5: Analyze asset and configuration information quality

Periodically, audit asset and configuration information to check on its quality. Review information quality based on these criteria:

- **Accuracy** — The documentation matches what truly exists
- **Completeness** — Partial information can be at least as damaging as no information, if its user assumes that he has complete information to base decisions upon
- **Timeliness** — Changes to the actual resources are documented immediately
- **Accessibility** — Current information is easily understandable and accessible to those required to use it

The frequency of your audits should depend upon the criticality of the information, frequency of changes, and the maturity of your organization's asset and configuration management discipline. If you have only begun to implement change management, audits should be more frequent.

Step 6: Reevaluate asset and configuration data and their update requirements

The system management discipline must evolve on a continuing basis, so it is not outpaced by the growth of the system, the IT organization, and the business as a whole.

At this stage, the results of the evaluation in the previous step should lead to action plans for improving information quality. What automation tools can help in the collection of configuration information? Should there be changes to the way information is gathered, stored, and made available to other people? How do you control the integrity of the configuration data on user workstations? These are just a few of the questions you'll need to answer at this phase of the discipline.

Process factors that are critical to the success of asset and configuration management are:

- **All changes are documented** — There is an unbreakable link between asset and configuration management and change management, because every change must end with a request to change all corresponding asset and configuration information. If this linkage is broken, then expect asset and configuration management to spend all its time trying to catch up with existing system configurations by way of repeated inspections and updates. Between update cycles, expect configuration data to be erroneous and a source of trouble to systems management disciplines that rely on it.

- **Information is kept current and accurate via regular audits** — Asset and configuration data loses its value the moment it becomes incorrect. Decisions based on incorrect information will most likely be wrong. It is vital that IT always has an accurate picture of what it must manage.

Data Requirements

The data to be maintained by asset and configuration management depends on the requirements of the other systems management disciplines, as in the following examples.

- **Service-level management:**
  - List of corporate assets by assigned owner, to know what assets need to be managed to fulfill system availability commitments
  - Configuration information by business applications, to know what system components need to be running during committed hours of operations
- **Problem management:**
  - Configuration information by user, to identify sources of problems
  - System configuration diagrams, to understand how reported problems might affect other users
- **Change management:**
  - System configuration diagrams, to determine how changes in one area might affect other system components
  - Configuration information by system component, to effectively plan for changes that might affect that component
- **Security management:**
  - System configuration diagram, to accurately track the location of sensitive assets and system components that process sensitive information
  - User assigned assets, to pinpoint responsibilities for safeguarding individual access to corporate assets
  - User profiles, to administer access control efficiently

Asset and configuration data may be grouped into five categories:

- **Physical data:**
  - Equipment installed, descriptions, serial numbers, and asset numbers
  - Equipment layout diagram
  - Power and air conditioning requirements

- Asset owner by department and assigned employee (all assets must have primary owners assigned)
- Spare and backup equipment and their storage locations
- **Network data:**
  - Network configuration diagram
  - Device addresses and port assignments
  - Cabling diagrams
  - Dial-up access numbers
- **Logical data:**
  - Application owners and user lists
  - Workstation users and their IDs
  - Databases and their locations
  - Servers and the resources they control or support
  - Application resource configuration diagrams
- **Hardware data:**
  - Warranty and vendor service information
  - Installed components (e.g., memory size, processor information, BIOS version)
  - Resource utilization (e.g., I/O interrupts used)
  - Administrative functions and their organization and configuration (e.g., PC BIOS configuration data)
- **Software data:**
  - Installed software, versions, and license information
  - Configuration parameters for each unique installation
  - Installed system utilities

Data-related factors that are critical to the success of asset and configuration management are:

- **All assets are properly inventoried and uniquely labeled —** There should be a corporate standard for labeling assets to uniquely identify each asset. We recommend that the asset label indicate the location of the asset by incorporating the department's initials (e.g., xxxxxx-ACC for assets located in the accounting department). Also, establish product codes corresponding to different types of assets (e.g., PCxxxxx-ACC for personal computers located in the accounting department).

Asset tags or labels should be placed where they are easily visible, usually below the product logo. They should be proportional to the size of the equipment. Finally, they should be tamper-proof or tamper-evident, and difficult to remove. These measures not only protect equipment from theft, but make it easier to physically locate assets quickly when they are needed.

- **All types of configuration data information available** — Again, it is critical that asset and configuration information be complete and thorough. Otherwise, users will have to manually extract the configuration information when needed. Since they cannot rely upon your database completely, they may not rely upon it at all.

Organization Requirements

End users have exceptional influence on whether asset and configuration management succeeds, so the support of senior management is essential. For example, if users remove or change asset labels when they transfer equipment, the labels immediately become inaccurate. If users change the configuration of their assigned PCs without informing IT, the configuration database maintained by the IT function will be wrong. Management should therefore incorporate asset protection and ownership responsibilities into every employee's conditions for employment.

A hierarchy of asset owners should be established to ensure that someone oversees the assets and asset owners under him. It is easiest to do this by user-unit-department-division-location, since every individual can easily identify to which group he belongs. This hierarchy can also be utilized to break up the periodic asset and configuration audit tasks, though it is still a good idea to have somebody from the IT organization to check on the authenticity of the data reported.

The following organizational factors are critical to the success of access and configuration management:

- **Owners assigned to assets** — Individual accountability is essential to provide true control over the use of your assets. One individual should be ultimately responsible for maintaining every asset, even those shared by many people. For example, department equipment such as fax machines or photocopy equipment might be assigned to the department administrative assistant. Usually, the location of the asset plays an important role in selecting its primary owner. Exceptions include IT equipment located throughout corporate premises but servicing a large set of users, for example, routers, hubs, or servers. In these instances, the asset should be secured in place or enclosed in a locked cabinet or room.

- **Changes to asset location, status, and ownership are authorized** — No IT-related equipment should be moved without prior approval from the change management process. Such changes would typically be requested via change request forms that indicate the final destination of the equipment, the reason for the change, and the approval of the user's immediate manager. This authorization step provides a level of safeguard against unnecessary, illegal, or undocumented changes that might impact the system as a whole.

Tools Requirements

Basic asset and configuration management requires an inventory database that allows easy searching of asset information. For configuration diagrams, use flowcharting or diagramming software to simplify inputs and updates. Use good quality tags and labels to ensure that they are not easily lost or destroyed.

Automation tools for obtaining system configuration data are being introduced, but they remain limited in scope and function. In many environments, we still recommend physically checking sensitive assets as the most accurate means of getting configuration data. We recognize that as more assets move farther away from IT's operations centers, this becomes increasingly taxing.

More of today's equipment provides electronic settings instead of mechanical switch settings whose status is difficult to examine remotely. PCs today are beginning to use tamper-resistant or tamper-evident casings to protect the installed hardware components from accidental or intentional modifications.

Among the numerous benefits of well-implemented asset and configuration disciplines are:

- **Loss of assets controlled if not eliminated** — Being able to secure assets begins with knowing what assets need to be protected, where they are located, and who has access to them. With a healthy asset and configuration management system in place, users are more aware of their individual duties and responsibilities towards those assets. Management is also more informed about the location and status of corporate assets, especially during employee changes or reassignments.
- **Improved ability to manage other systems management disciplines, especially problem and change management** — With accurate system configuration information, problem management goes more smoothly, since solutions are based on more accurate information. For example, while trying to fix a network access problem, accurate labeling and documentation reduces the chances that a technician will pull the wrong cable and cause an even greater network outage. Changes can now be better planned, since change evaluators will have access to current information about the resources that will be affected by the changes. System security can be more easily maintained, since the security administrator, who also knows what workstations each user works with, and how users gain access to the applications they need.

▶ Availability Management

It is essential that all systems management disciplines function effectively together. Each has a role to play in achieving service-level targets, but operating independently of each other, they can do more harm than good. Each discipline has its own set of objectives and targets, which must be balanced with those of the other disciplines.

For example, the objective of problem management is to resolve problems as quickly as possible. Often, this requires emergency changes to system resources. But if emergency changes do not go through the change management process, they can lead to more problems in the future. So there must be a compromise — problem management must ensure that emergency changes are documented and submitted to change management for post-implementation analysis, while change management must allow emergency changes to take place without the usual approvals and pre-implementation planning.

Since individual systems management targets are oriented towards their own disciplines, it is easy to lose sight of the larger objective of system availability and end user service quality. Herein lies the need to have an overall view of all the systems management disciplines and how they impact the overall availability of the system. This function or role belongs to the availability manager, using a process called availability management.

Process Requirements

The process of availability management begins with an understanding of the service levels committed to end users. The availability measures achieved are tracked and remedial measures are defined to ensure that the targets are achieved.

Step 1: Define a plan to achieve availability targets

First, gain a thorough understanding of the Service Level Agreement and the targets it mandates. With this knowledge, the availability manager can assess where the IT organization currently stands with respect to these targets.

Next, draw up a plan for bringing the IT organization close to achieving those targets, prioritizing critical areas requiring immediate attention. Assign target dates, owners, and resources. The plan can incorporate the system availability techniques that will be discussed in the following chapters.

Step 2: Track availability targets and their achievement

Monitor critical system components for their availability. Record all outages, including information on what happened, when it happened, what was affected, the duration of the outage, and the impact on end users. Your objective is to prevent the same outages from happening again. To accomplish this, perform post-outage analysis to determine root cause. Knowing the symptoms or conditions prior to the occurrence of the outage will also help in the prevention of future outages.

Step 3: Analyze and report on availability achievements

Analyze the data you have gathered for trends and statistics. Often, small problems lead to big problems if the small ones are left unresolved. Examine trend reports for failure patterns, common points of failures, and critical contributors to the problem.

Discuss these reports with selected users and members of the IT organization: they may be able to provide information that has not been captured by the reports. Repetitive outages should be highlighted and given greater focus.

To justify new resources for addressing these outages, report on the business impact of outages. This impact assessment can cover missed business opportunities, lost user productivity, lost IT staff productivity, and any damage to physical or information assets.

Step 4: Update availability plan

As a result of the preceding findings, identify measures to improve system availability, and incorporate them into a new plan. Such measures could include:

- Configuration improvements
- Application deployment and design improvements
- Data placement and use improvements
- Implementation of techniques for higher availability (as discussed in the following chapters)
- Improvements to other systems management processes
- Improvements to the IT organization

Process factors critical to the success of availability management are:

- **Outage and root cause analysis is done** — Outage analysis is essential to prevent future availability problems. Many organizations fail to pin down the causes of problems because they concentrate on the symptoms of the problem rather than on the root cause of the outage. Hardware will fail, users will err, and software will crash, but the system does not necessarily have to have an outage if it has been designed to tolerate failures well.

Let's discuss an example. A system designed to run continuously 24 hours a day, 7 days a week suddenly shuts down. A one-hour power outage occurred 30 minutes ago, and a generator designed to operate for two hours stopped functioning because it ran out of fuel. What is the root cause of the system outage? Many people blame the power failure. But the root cause of the outage is really the lack of fuel for the generator — the person in charge of checking fuel levels failed to do so the previous day. One remedial measure might be to have another person double-check the fuel supply regularly. Another might be to choose a generator that can automatically send low-fuel alerts to appropriate administrators.

As shown above, good outage and root cause analysis can identify the true cause of the outage, one that could have been avoided but was not. Nobody could have prevented the original power outage, because the electric company, a third party, controls the power supply. But a generator was put in place precisely to prevent power outages from affecting the system. The generator running out of fuel could have been prevented, but was not.

- **Other systems management disciplines should be governed by the availability management process** — Availability management serves to check and balance the performance of all the other systems management disciplines. Without this factor, it is likely that systems management disciplines will fail to reach their objective of improving overall availability.

Data Requirements

Much of the data required by availability management is generated by the other systems management disciplines. Specifically, the trends and summary reports of the other disciplines are important inputs for evaluating total system health:

- **Service-level management** provides:
  - Service Level Agreement
  - Service-level attainment

- **Problem management** provides:
  - Problem trends and statistics
  - Root causes of problems
- **Change management** provides:
  - Summary of implemented changes
- **Security management** provides:
  - Summary of security violations

Additionally, information on any high availability features in installed products can help you identify new measures for improving system availability.

Data factors critical to the success of availability management are:

- **Availability of data when needed** — Information needed from the other systems management disciplines should be on hand.
- **Currency of data provided by the other systems management disciplines** — Obviously, good decisions can only come from information that is complete and current, so updated information should always be available.

Organization Requirements

The function of availability management is best assigned to an individual who is neither the IT manager nor the CIO. Availability management must be done on an ongoing basis, not just tackled when someone has spare time. Bear in mind that the availability manager acts as the focal point for all issues relating to the availability and stability of all IT services.

Having a dedicated availability manager eliminates a fragmented approach to availability management, ensures consistent reporting of availability achievement, ensures that problem trends are being addressed, and provides accountability for the system's overall availability record. Having a dedicated availability manager also provides advantages to the IT manager or CIO. For example, the availability manager can focus on these major areas:

- Defining long term strategies for the IT organization
- Developing new services in support of the business

- Setting performance targets for the IT staff
- Determining system capacity requirements

In addition to these high-level responsibilities, the availability manager is also responsible for:

- Implementing the availability management process
- Ensuring availability of all services provided
- Establishing effective communication and reporting significant availability issues
- Evaluating systems management processes for effectiveness and efficiency

Organizational issues critical to the success of availability management are:

- **Availability manager should have management authority** — Because of the sensitive and managerial nature of his role, the availability manager should be at the same level as or slightly lower than the IT manager, reporting directly to the CIO. He must be able to:
  - Influence changes in policies and procedures affecting the systems management disciplines
  - Coordinate cross-departmental resources
  - Commit a plan and the resources needed to achieve it
  - Monitor business process effectiveness and efficiency
- **Availability manager should be given management jurisdiction** — The availability manager will act to oversee the performance of all systems management disciplines, settling disputes that arise among them. It is thus essential that he has the right to decide on the actions of all process owners. He should not need permission from the IT manager or CIO to make key decisions.

Tools Requirements

No special tools are required by the availability manager, except those needed to access the information generated by the other systems management disciplines.

Benefits

There are at least two benefits to be realized from well-implemented availability management.

- **Greater focus and attention is put on the achievement of system availability and service-level targets** — With availability management in place, the IT organization is better directed towards the ultimate objective of end-user satisfaction. Without a dedicated availability management process in place, the IT organization usually ends up relying on special projects to address user satisfaction (e.g., user satisfaction surveys). All too often, these fail to have lasting impact, since there is rarely sufficient follow-through activity.

- **More efficient use of IT resources towards achievement of the service-level targets** — Availability management deals with requirements for managing all the systems management disciplines in a unified manner, focusing on outage prevention from the user's point of view. It acts to coordinate the different resources focused on specific systems management disciplines, ensuring that what one does is not undone by another. The end result is that the interaction between the systems management disciplines is enhanced.

From Centralized to Distributed Computing Environments

▶ Systems Management Disciplines

Many systems management disciplines were crafted during the mainframe-centric era. Because of their close ties with "big iron," advocates of the shift away from centralized computing also abandoned systems management disciplines, believing their new world order would not need them. They were wrong.

Today, we see distributed computing environments being challenged by the same problems that confronted mainframe-centric IT organizations — how to satisfy users, how to handle problems, managing changes, securing the computing environment, etc. In fact, the problem is even more complex, because the resources that need to be managed are physically farther apart and often controlled by people outside the IT organization.

We are not about to abandon distributed computing simply because centralized computing is easier to manage. Distributed computing arose from a real need by users to have greater access to corporate data using software applications that can be developed rapidly, even by the users themselves. We must find a way to manage the IT infrastructure of today — many computers connected together to form one giant computer system spread across different locations.

▶ The Centralized Computing Environment

In a centralized, mainframe-centric computing environment, users have access to the computer system via dumb terminals. The dumb terminal has no data processing capability. Its only function is to receive keyboard input from the users, pass it on to the mainframe computer, and then display the resulting data. When a terminal breaks, the user can simply go to another terminal and continue working. The IT organization can send a technician to replace the defective terminal simply by transferring the communication cable to the replacement unit — no complicated reconfigurations or system settings must be recreated.

In this environment, all data is stored in a central computing facility. User applications also reside on this equipment. No data or application ever resides on the user's terminal. In terms of security, the IT organization must only physically enclose the system in a secured room (called the glass house because it is usually constructed of glass to showcase the corporate computing asset), and back up the data daily. Management can sleep soundly, knowing that all-important data is protected from harm.

Because hardly anything ever goes wrong with the user's terminal or remote printer, the IT staff spends its days in the comfort of their own space. If there is ever a problem with the system, they can just skip over to the next room and check it out for themselves.

However, when things *do* go wrong, the entire business is affected. Since everything resides on the main computer, if it goes down, nobody can do anything that requires access to the computer. These downtimes are sometimes called "computer holidays" — no work at work. The cost to fix mainframe hardware problems can also be extremely high, unless the system is covered by a cost-effective maintenance agreement with the vendor that sold the equipment.

The Distributed Computing Environment

In a distributed computing environment, users have their own workstations, usually a personal computer connected to the corporate network. Users can run their own software, accessing corporate data whenever needed. Corporate data once presented in dull, boring, green numbers can now appear in different fonts, colors, and sizes, with graphics and sound if so desired. Users no longer have to wait endlessly for IT systems programmers to develop their applications — novice programmers can do it for them on their own computers, using shrink-wrapped tools available in the shopping mall.

In this environment, corporate data and applications are distributed all over the network. Some of them are in the old mainframe computer, aptly renamed as the corporate server, while some reside in departmental servers, user workstations, or on diskettes inside desk drawers and users' shirt pockets. When things go wrong, the whole business is rarely affected. In fact, one user's problem is often unnoticed by those around him. Also, the cost to fix a problem with the user's computer or a company server is usually trivial compared with the eye-popping expenses of mainframe repairs.

But management will have many sleepless nights in this computing environment. They know that if a major disaster occurs to their office facility, many users will suffer because the data they need to run the business has not been adequately backed up. In a major disaster, they can only restore data down to the departmental server level, assuming they had the foresight to plan for backup and recovery. They had no foresight (or the money and expertise) to implement some form of backup mechanism that covered all the user workstations.

Many things can go wrong in many different places. They may happen at the user's workstation because his software was hit by a computer virus. They may be at the departmental server that was accidentally shut down when somebody tripped over its power cables. They may even be in a different country on a user's notebook computer that cannot connect to the company's server via the Internet. The IT staff find themselves spending a good amount of time traveling or desperately trying to resolve the problem over the phone to avoid that long and tiring trip to the remote user location.

Systems Management in Today's Computing Environment

Today's computing environment is a mix of the old and new, a combination of centralized and distributed computing. This calls for a different approach to systems management, one that recognizes the challenges of managing remote resources.

Defining Appropriate Functions and Control

The challenge of systems management today is simply a matter of determining the best way to deploy the systems management function and control. This placement of management function and control can take different forms.

Centralized management and control

This is the traditional deployment strategy for systems management — it is most suitable for highly centralized computing environments. All systems management functions are performed by a central committee composed primarily of IT staff. Remote resources are all managed from the IT data center.

Centralized management, distributed control

All decisions about systems management are made by the IT organization. However, implementation of management functions at locations outside of the main IT data center is handled by autonomous agents or mini-IT groups assigned to each department or function.

Systems management agents are assigned to handle most day-to-day tasks of systems management. They must only consult the central IT organization about issues that may impact other functions or departments. This arrangement can be faster and more responsive. However, the coordination required between remote agents and centralized IT strains the management abilities of many IT organizations.

Distributed management and control

All decisions and actions pertaining to systems management are in the hands of autonomous groups or individuals at each remote location. The central IT organization provides no coordination.

Rarely seen today, this approach is difficult to implement successfully unless the remote locations themselves have purely autonomous information systems with little sharing of data or applications throughout the enterprise. Today's reality is that there is greater interaction between different enterprise computing resources — most critical business information is used across the entire enterprise.

Whatever systems management deployment strategy is chosen, systems management tasks must be automated as much as possible. The advantages of removing human intervention include elimination of human error, improved consistency, tireless implementation of activities, and the ability to schedule tasks any time of the night or day.

Choosing a Deployment Strategy

Bearing in mind the four elements of any management system (data, tools, process, and organization), your choice of deployment strategy will depend on the following elements:

Capability to manage remote resources

To manage remote resources effectively and efficiently, you must design them to be manageable in the first place. Here are three guidelines for determining the manageability of a given resource:

- **Resource status can be queried remotely** — You need not physically inspect a resource to determine its current state. A simple example is determining whether a resource is powered on — older equipment gives you no way to determine this remotely. Other vital resource status conditions include: is the resource operational? Online? In error? Overloaded?

  As for personal computers, until recently, most could not provide configuration information remotely, unless a technician shut down the computer and viewed BIOS data, or even opened up the case and examined its internal components. This has changed — most of today's better business PCs can be polled remotely for important data such as installed system memory, attached peripherals, and hardware versions.

- **Management information is maintained by the resource itself** — Remote management is simplified if certain information about the resource is kept by the resource itself. Data such as resource configuration information, operational status, and features and options are essential to systems management. If information about resources is maintained by a separate system, chances are this information is not current, complete, or easily accessible. Take a look at your existing computer inventory database and judge for yourself how accurate its information is. Imagine how much better it could be if you can directly interrogate the remote resources for their latest configuration information.

- **Resource status can be changed remotely** — Remote systems management can be made more effective if resources can be reconfigured or redefined remotely. Obstacles to this are mechanical switches, hardwired settings, and cabling.

Skills availability at remote locations

If remote locations have people with the skills to manage their resources, consider using these skilled people to distribute your management workload. These people are often non-IT professionals who have learned enough about technology to become the local "IT guru," to whom everyone in a department runs for help. You might formally assign certain systems management tasks to these people, so they become, in essence, your representative. Bear in mind, though, that this strategy has risks, such as:

- **Demoralization** on the part of the new representative, who may have added workload and responsibilities that are not part of their original job descriptions

- **Negative impact on the productivity** of the new representatives, who are then prevented from performing their original responsibilities

- **Lesser quality of work** with respect to the systems management tasks, since these would have to be performed along with the person's current job responsibilities

To avoid these consequences, you might prefer to assign a dedicated resource from the central IT organization, instead of appointing someone from the remote organization.

In an environment where the users themselves are highly skilled, certain systems management tasks can be passed on to them. These might include regular data backups, computer virus checking, and file-level security maintenance. The only issue — a difficult one — is to ensure that users diligently perform the tasks you've assigned to them.

In short, only plan for remote resource management if your remote organizations have sufficient skills and people with sufficient reliability.

Performance impact of managing remote resources centrally

As more remote resources are deployed, managing them uses more network bandwidth. For example, monitoring systems can check the status of an individual networked PC and server by pinging it, with hardly any noticeable effect on network performance. But if you have a thousand systems to check, and you must update status information every 15 minutes, you will begin to experience noticeable network slowdowns.

When systems management functions are distributed to the remote resources, their performance speed can often increase, since the tasks are performed close to the resources. For example, backing up data on a server using an attached tape drive is much faster than backing it up to a central server, since data backed up locally doesn't travel across the network. Localizing tasks such as this frees up network bandwidth for more critical applications, improving system performance.

The need for greater security and control

Distributing systems management tasks widely to remote locations tends to make systems less secure and more difficult to control, since more external variables come into play. In security management, for example, if password management is delegated to every user, the risk increases that users will select poor passwords, fail to keep them confidential, and leave them unchanged for too long. Thus, we recommend that the central IT organization retain responsibility for sensitive systems management functions, such as:

- Security administration
- Data backup and recovery
- Change control and administration
- Network administration

Physical proximity of resources to each other

The more physically distant resources are, the harder they are to manage centrally. If remote resources require on-site maintenance or repair, the central IT organization would expend a lot of time and energy getting the job done. Even from a network standpoint, distance tends to be correlated with workload — the more network devices a message or command must traverse, the more slowly it arrives, and the more network bandwidth it requires.

▶ Developing a Deployment Strategy

Here are strategies you can employ when deploying your own systems management infrastructure.

Management by Exception

Repetitive tasks can be distributed to the remote locations and executed locally for speed and efficiency. Whenever predefined limits are exceeded, the remote systems managers alert the central systems manager. In this way, events or conditions that may have an impact upon the availability of the enterprise system are known to the central management function.

With this strategy, central management must define the limits or thresholds remote system managers must watch. Hence, a certain level of control is retained centrally.

This strategy can be applied whether the remote systems management functions are performed by people or by automated systems management agents. For example, you can form mini-IT groups that will run the day-to-day operations of remote systems. They can be mandated to report to the central IT organization such things as the number of problems encountered over a given period of time, the problems that remain unresolved, and summary system performance data. The central IT organization would provide quality control for the support provided by the remote IT organizations, ensuring that it meets enterprise-wide standards. In this way, flexibility is achieved at the remote locations, but quality control is ensured for the entire organization.

As an example of the use of automated systems management agents, in an environment where multiple LANs are connected to an enterprise backbone, each LAN can have a system that monitors for errors and automatically performs recovery from minor problems. Whenever errors reach a certain frequency, the system alerts the centralized network monitoring system, which can then perform more thorough diagnosis or corrective action.

Policy-Based Management

Policy-based management refers to the identification of targets and guidelines the remote systems management agents will follow. These guidelines should be followed *to the letter*, thereby maintaining the quality of service and system performance required for any effective enterprise-wide systems management.

When it comes to decentralizing the systems management functions, you can hand over certain systems management tasks to the users themselves, asking them to abide by certain established corporate policies regarding managing their own workstations. For example, a company policy data backup can be established, placing the task of making regular backups in the hands of the users, and eliminating the need for a single corporate backup system that might be expensive and difficult to implement.

Many tools for systems management allow for policy-based management. For example, password management systems can be run at the user's workstation, using security policies defined and distributed centrally. This eliminates the need for a single security system to monitor every workstation from a central location. Instead, the central system can simply poll each workstation daily, asking the local security monitoring system for status reports, including the number of invalid logon attempts, password naming standards compliance, etc. Distributed security systems can also be configured to alert the central security system if a threshold is reached, as discussed in the strategy of management by exception.

Standardization of Performance Data

If many mini-IT groups manage your distributed systems, make sure everyone follows the same guidelines for reporting to the central IT organization. This simplifies the task of correlating individual reports and understanding enterprise-wide performance. It also simplifies communication between autonomous units. Begin with a common dictionary of systems management, and then agree on the format of reports, their frequency, and breadth of coverage.

When contemplating automated systems management, ensure that the deployed systems management tools all use the same language for communicating system management data. For example, do not install products that work under CA Unicenter in *some* systems, while using Tivoli software on *others*, as this may prevent you from getting data from the two to work together seamlessly.

Accountability of the Distributed Systems Manager

Emphasize the accountability of the distributed systems managers or agents over their assigned areas of responsibility. Make sure that distributed agents know that if anything goes wrong, they will be held liable for the tasks assigned to them.

Central Definition of Systems Management Architectures

Central IT should define a systems management architecture or infrastructure for use throughout the enterprise. What operating system should the systems management tools run on? Where should it reside? Will it be centralized or distributed? What systems management disciplines will be automated? Which will remain manual? These are but a few questions that must be answered by the central IT organization and communicated to all distributed IT group or systems management agent.

Process Ownership

An organization must be in place for performing all of these systems management processes. There should be individuals whose main responsibility is to make sure that the systems management processes are performed properly from start to finish. These process owners should review the quality of performance of the systems management discipline assigned to them, whether they work in the operations group, the technical support group, or elsewhere. They should be empowered to manage staff of each function within the IT group. Hence, people within the IT organization report to either their functional managers or to the process owners.

For example, a member of the technical support group may report to the technical support manager for the performance of his duties, but may also report to the problem management process owner for activities pertaining to the resolution of problems. This emphasis on functional as well as process-based responsibilities results in what is known as a matrix organization, where an individual no longer reports just to one manager. This matrix organization is essential for preventing the functional narrow-mindedness prevalent in many IT organizations. It is also vital to process-related disciplines, since processes invariably encompass many different functions and people.

▶ Summary

Systems management is an integral part of any high availability system, and a necessary ingredient in achieving higher availability. The systems management disciplines learned from the mainframe-centric world are needed more than ever in today's distributed computing environment. Without systems management:

- Users will encounter many outages, even with the best hardware and software configurations
- The people factor will become a significant cause of outages
- IT staff will spend most of its time solving problems, leading to ongoing crisis management

With an effective systems management in place:

- Users may never experience an outage, even with merely adequate hardware and software
- The people factor will be less of a concern
- T staff will spend more of their time designing new applications and anticipating potential problems — in other words, they can manage proactively

As the systems management principle goes:

There are no technical solutions to management problems,
but there may be management solutions to technical problems.

Techniques That Address Multiple Availability Requirements

▶ Redundancy

A into A and B where A = B and either A or B may be used

Redundancy is a technique whereby a system component is duplicated and either of the two may be used at any one time. Since two identical components are now online, the system can continue to function when one of them fails. In fact, there will be no impact to the system operation when that happens. Redundancy enhances:

- **Reliability** — Failures are masked from the users — they experience no outage, and their systems appear more reliable.
- **Recoverability** — Error conditions can be corrected almost instantaneously, since the redundant component is automatically used in place of the failed one. Virtually instant recovery makes redundancy a powerful way to improve system availability.

- **Serviceability** — When a failure occurs on one redundant system component, a repair can be performed while the good redundant component continues to function, eliminating the need for a system shutdown, and simplifying service.
- **Manageability** — Even though there is an additional component to manage, there should be fewer outages. The overall result should be a system that is more manageable, not less.

Hardware Redundancy Examples

- **Dual power supplies** can operate at the same time in a high availability computer server. If one power supply fails, the other continues to operate, and the system is unaffected. This solution is common in popular computer servers. When evaluating systems incorporating dual power supplies, choose one that permits "hot swapping" of the failed power supply without a power down. Not only does this make the system more available, it simplifies scheduling a repair, since the work can be done at any time. Each redundant power supply should have its own set of power cables, so you can connect them to two different power sources if so desired. This further reduces the chances of system outage.
- **Dual network interface cards (NICs)** can be found in high availability computer servers designed to function as file or application servers. If a NIC fails, built-in failover software automatically deactivates it, switching network traffic to the alternate NIC. The rerouting happens almost instantaneously, so the user is unaware that a problem has occurred.
- **Disk mirroring and duplexing** means that two hard disk drives store identical sets of data. Available in Windows NT 4.0 Server, Windows 2000 Server, NetWare 4.x and 5.x, and other network operating systems, this data duplication is performed automatically. All write operations to one disk are performed also on the mirror disk drive. When the primary drive fails, the switchover to the backup drive takes place automatically.
- **Redundant Array of Inexpensive Disks (RAID)** combines several independent storage devices into one storage subsystem that delivers data to client systems as if it was a single storage device,

but typically with greater performance or reliability. How the data is stored in each of the disks defines the type of RAID implementation of the storage subsystem, as discussed next.

- **RAID-0** — In RAID-0, data is spread across all disks in the storage array sequentially, with no mirroring or parity information. Performance is enhanced, since the workload is spread across all disks, and all disks can be active simultaneously. However, RAID-0 does not improve availability, and may in fact weaken it. If one disk in the array fails, data stored on all other disks in the array becomes bad too.

- **RAID-1** — RAID-1 is also known as mirroring. Data in one drive is duplicated in another disk in the array. As long as one good copy of the mirrored data exists, you can deliver continuous data availability to the user. The disadvantage of RAID-1 is its cost — you must allot twice as much storage capacity. Also, storage system write performance is affected, since each data write operation must be performed at least twice — more, if you choose to create additional mirrors of your data. Read performance, however, may be improved with RAID-1, since the read data request may be broadcasted to all drives, with the first available drive providing the data even if mirrored copies are still busy.

- **RAID-2** — With RAID-2, data is stored across the disks bit by bit, with extra disks holding check bits that make it possible to verify, correct, and recover from errors. If a primary disk is damaged, the check disks are examined to reconstruct the data. This is similar to the use of ECC code in computer memory devices. The disadvantage of RAID-2 is that it requires extra disk drives to maintain the error correction information, resulting in a more expensive storage subsystem. Also, all disk drives must be accessed to retrieve a piece of data, potentially slowing down the read or write process. Lastly, there is still only one copy of the data stored, so true redundancy is not achieved.

- **RAID-3** — With RAID-3, data is also stored across many disks, but on a byte-by-byte basis. Parity or check information is stored on a dedicated disk, so that it can protect up to four data disks. In essence, RAID-3's overhead is twenty percent. If an error occurs on one drive, the parity information is used to restore the data. This implementation also allows for hot swapping of drives during maintenance. RAID-3 can provide greater throughput by reading or writing to multiple drives simultaneously. Because of its approach to data storage, performance of a RAID-3 device slows down considerably when many small data transfers are taking place.

- **RAID-4** — Similar to RAID-3, RAID-4 stores the data across many disks, but with one data block per disk, so that only one disk needs to be accessed for a read request. A parity disk is still maintained. This means there is the capability for parallel reads, but writes must all access the parity drive, creating the potential for a bottleneck. Unlike RAID-3, rebuilding of data cannot be done on line. For this reason, RAID-4 is seldom supported in modern RAID implementations.

- **RAID-5** — In RAID-5, data is stored across the drives of the array in segments, and parity information is maintained. Instead of using a dedicated disk to store the parity information, however, RAID-5 dedicates the equivalent of one entire disk for storing check data, but distributes the parity information across all the drives in the group. The primary benefit of the RAID-5 distributed check-data approach is that it permits multiple write operations to take place simultaneously. It also allows multiple reads to take place simultaneously and is efficient in handling small amounts of information. RAID-5 is best suited for applications that manipulate small data sizes, such as transaction processing applications.

Software Redundancy Examples

- **Duplicate applications stores** can be configured. Copies of all applications, resident on a separate host or server that is ready to run if the primary copy goes down. Switchover to the backup copies should be automatic and transparent to users. To simplify the creation of redundant application stores, separate data from executables. This helps to ensure that application files do not change as they are used, since no dynamic components are stored within them. For instance, in Microsoft Access database applications, data tables are normally stored with the queries, forms, and reports — when changes to the data occur, the entire application file is updated. To make it easy to convert such applications into redundant copies, you can split the database into a front-end section that incorporates queries, forms, and reports, and a back end section with only the tables. This way, only back-end files change while the front-end database files remain static until design changes are made.

- **TCP/IP-based Internet communications** are a perfect example of redundancy at work. Because TCP/IP communications largely ignore the type of network connection, focusing solely on destination IP addresses, one transaction can pass through a set of network components that may be totally different from the components that delivered the previous transaction. This switching between paths occurs without user intervention, effectively creating a network with a virtually infinite number of redundant paths.

- **Mirrored databases** can be configured to enable applications to access any redundant copy depending on network availability and other criteria. Mirroring requires significant network bandwidth because every data update must be performed on the mirrored copy as well. Also, frequent data updates make synchronization of the primary and the mirror databases difficult. Database mirroring may be supported by the operating system. For example, IBM's AIX and its Logical Volume Manager can create and maintain up to three copies of a logical volume.

Environmental Redundancy Example

Dual power connectors are used in IBM mainframes to isolate servers from potential power supply problems. Two independent power supplies provide power to the computer with their own set of power cords. You then connect these power cords to two separate electricity sources, ideally coming from different power grids. When one power grid goes down, the other power supply continues to function — unless, of course, the outage impacts both power grids to which your system is connected.

Critical Success Factors

- **Automatic load-shifting** — In a redundant configuration, one component should automatically take over the load of the other component when a failure occurs.
- **Identical redundant components** — Redundant components should be identical to each other, making it transparent to the rest of the system which of the two components is actually functioning. In normal operations, when both components are functioning on line, the load can be shared between the two.

▶ Backup of Critical Resources

A into A (primary) and B (backup) where A = B and B is used when A is unavailable

Backup is the technique whereby a system component is duplicated and the backup is put in reserve or standby, to be used when the primary fails. Unlike redundancy, the user may still experience an outage — the challenge is to minimize the time it takes to switch to the backup component, thereby minimizing the length of the outage. Backup enhances:

- **Reliability** — When a problem occurs, users might only experience an outage of short duration. If a system was designed to gracefully recover from a fault, users may merely notice a prolonged response time.
- **Recoverability** — The more recent the backup copy, the less impact the recovery process will have on users.
- **Serviceability** — The primary system component can be serviced while the backup continues to provide user access, eliminating the need to schedule maintenance during off hours.
- **Manageability** — The backup technique may negatively impact manageability, since more components must be managed. But, if the technique is implemented correctly, the impact should be marginal, since the backup and primary components are the same. The long-term improvements in system availability should lessen overall IT staff workload.

Methods of Backup

There are different levels of implementation of backup:

- **One-to-one** — One backup is made for each primary system component. This level is the most expensive to implement if you want to protect many primary components, but is effective in preventing an outage.
- **One-to-many** — One backup is shared by many primary system components. This level is less costly to implement but is ineffective if more than one primary goes down.
- **Many-to-many** — Many backups are shared by many primary system components. This level is the most cost-effective implementation since it can handle as many primary outages as there are backups. It is not as limited in capability as the one-to-many and not as expensive as one-to-one. It is more complex to implement than the other two types of implementations.

There are also different types of backups, differing in their availability in case of an outage:

- **Hot backup** — The backup is configured and installed, ready to run whenever needed. This is almost equivalent to having a redundant system component, except that here the backup component is not actually operational until activated. This type of backup must be configured as closely as possible to the primary system. For example, if it is a data backup, then the data should be as current as possible. Obviously, this type of backup is the most expensive and complicated to implement.
- **Cold backup** — The backup is available, but it still must be configured and installed before it can be activated. This type of backup is easier to implement and maintain than a hot backup. And an easily overlooked advantage is that the spare is readily available — no need to go through the hassles of purchasing a replacement, especially outside of business hours. For data, cold backups can be considered as those stored in magnetic media such as tape, since these still have to be taken from the tape vault, mounted onto the tape drive, and read by the system. The data they contain is also only as current as the last time that the tape backup was updated.

- **Supplier backup** — The backup is not on hand, rather, you maintain a standing agreement with the supplier to provide a backup in case of an outage. This is the least expensive type of backup — you don't need to invest in anything until the need arises. For system components that are non-critical or have especially low failure rates, this type of backup may be suitable. It eliminates the problem of looking for a supplier when you need the backup. However, its effectiveness in reducing outage duration is low because of the potential delays in the actual purchasing, delivery, and installation of the component. This backup technique is most applicable to hardware resources.

Hardware Backup Examples

- **Backup of sensitive hardware components,** that is, system components that are prone to failure. Most of these components can be cold-backup types or even supplier backups if their criticality is low. Depending on how your system is designed, these components are usually those that: have mechanical parts; were manufactured with less than ideal quality standards (i.e., non-branded or clone equipment); are older; or are used in extreme environmental conditions. Examples include printers, diskettes, hard disks, memory modules, graphics cards, network interface cards, network cabling, network hubs and switches, power supplies, and modems.
- **Standby Recovery Server (Compaq example)** is an implementation whereby two servers share the same set of storage systems. If the primary server fails, then the storage system is automatically switched over to the backup server, which starts up and brings the system back on line in minutes.

Software Backup Examples

- **Software warehouse** is a safe location where you can keep fresh copies of software applications, preferably preconfigured to work in the current system. These copies should be tested to be virus-free and at the current version or release level in use. If the system goes down and must be restored to a different computer system, a software warehouse will go a long way toward reducing the outage duration. We recommend that every time you roll out a new application, you store a copy of the code in a safe location. This software warehouse can also include copies of the configuration files or system parameters in both software and hard copy version. Think of software warehousing as data backups specifically tailored for applications. Though some might argue that system backups would address this need, we still advocate using software warehouses to add an extra level of insurance.

- **Registry backup feature of Windows 9x and Windows 2000** protects the system registry, a configuration file where all hardware, operating system, and program parameters are stored in a computer running Windows 95, 98, or Windows 2000. If this registry information is corrupted, you might otherwise have to reinstall the operating system. To safeguard against this, Windows automatically keeps backup copies of the system registry — one based on the first successful system startup after installation, and another created after the most recent successful system startup. If the registry is corrupted, you can restore it using first the most recent successful startup copy, and if still unsuccessful, by using the registry version during the first successful startup.

- **Data backups** are essential because data is the hardest asset to recover if lost, especially in very complex business operations. Most if not all IT organizations have some form of data backup. Here are some approaches:

  - **Centralized backup** — Data backups are performed on a central system by getting all the data from the remote sources on a regular basis. The advantage of this approach is greater control — you can ensure that backups are being done regularly, and that they are all stored securely. The disadvantage is the strain on the network bandwidth when backups are run. This strain can be eased by the use of faster, more reliable central data backup devices.

  - **Distributed backup** — Data backups are done and stored in multiple remote workstations or locations. In this approach, it is up to the remote locations to initiate and manage their backups, freeing network bandwidth for other processes. It is also cheaper to implement this method because hardware and software costs are usually lower for smaller systems found at remote or workgroup locations. The disadvantage — it is difficult to ensure that quality backups are done regularly.

- **Hierarchical backup** — This approach provides a happy compromise between distributed and centralized backup. Here, frequent backups (e.g., daily) are done at the remote or distributed stations, which also send their data backups to a central location less frequently (e.g., weekly). Updating the central backup can be done during off-peak hours, thereby preventing the loss of valuable network bandwidth. Backup systems that implement this approach are also known as distributed storage managers (e.g., Adstar's ADSM).

These types of backup systems also implement some form of automatic selection of backup media depending on the currency of the data that is backed up. Data that changes often is left in high-speed storage devices such as high-performance hard disks. Data that is older or changes less frequently is stored in slower, less costly storage devices such as optical disks, QIC, DAT, AIT and other magnetic tape media.

IT Operations Backup Examples

- **Personnel backup** — *people need to be backed up, too.* Make sure more than one person has the critical skills needed to ensure that IT operations continue unhampered despite the loss or absence of key individuals. Consider operations staff first, then systems programmers and analysts, help desk staff, and systems administrators.

- **Service provider backup** should be in place. Most IT organizations rely on the availability of service engineers from vendors they purchased their software or equipment from. Worst off are those with no formal maintenance agreements, even with primary service providers. When a disaster affecting multiple companies occurs, those companies will be last on line for service.

- **Operations manuals** can answer questions about critical procedures for running your IT infrastructure. Documentation may be one of the hardest tasks for any IT organization, especially those in environments facing both downsizing and constant systems upgrades. But this is vital to any organization that wants to survive not just a major disaster, but even minor outages as well. What are the procedures for bringing up a system and shutting it down? What does the system configuration look like? What are the commands for resetting a network resource? What are the system administrator user IDs and passwords? Get the picture?

Critical Success Factors

All of the factors described in the following subsections are critical to the success of your backup strategies.

Currency of backup

More current backups lead to shorter outages and less overall impact on users. Unfortunately, the more current the backup is, the more expensive and complex it is to implement, with respect to finances, labor, and resource utilization. The update schedule you choose should depend upon:

- Frequency of changes
- Criticality of changes (e.g., data accuracy)
- Risk of loss (e.g., reliability of storage media) or susceptibility to failure

Automated updating of backups

Build a data backup system that runs with as little human intervention as possible. This largely removes the possibility of human error or negligence from the equation, improving the likelihood that proper backups will be performed on the proper schedule.

Isolation of backup from primary

Locate your primary and backup system components as far away from each other as possible, so any physical damage to the primary system is less likely to affect the backup. Separation is especially important in reducing the risks associated with natural and man-made calamities. For example, if the primary server location burns down and the backup server and backup tapes are in the same room, you lose both resources and any chances of recovery. However, keep in mind that the greater the distance between the primary and the backup, the harder it is to make them equivalent.

Backup and restore procedure review and testing

It is easy to assume that you have a working backup until you actually need it, and discover that it is useless. This has happened many times to companies, especially with backup data stored in removable media.

Regularly test your backups to ensure that your procedures for creating and maintaining them are actually effective. Perform these reviews whenever you make significant changes to the system. The true test of your own site's ability to recover from an outage and restore normal operations using a backup is to perform unannounced failure simulations.

Now is also a good time to evaluate your choice of backup media for reliability.

Generations of backups

Especially for data and software warehouses, you should retain multiple generations of backups — different copies of different ages. Sometimes data corruption or loss is not detected immediately. If only one backup copy is kept, even *that* backup may have corrupted data. Also, backup storage media may fail, so having multiple backups is an insurance against this problem. Our recommendation for having multiple generations of backups is to use the grandfather-father-son methodology:

- **Daily backups** are made, with backups for each day kept intact until the following week, when the backups are overwritten. Label each backup by the day of the week (e.g., Monday, Tuesday, etc.).

- **Every end of the week,** weekly backups are made. You retain four weekly backups, one for each week of the month. Next month, you begin overwriting these backups, once a week, starting with the oldest.
- **Every start of the month,** monthly backups are made. You can keep as many monthly backups as you desire.

At the start of implementation of this methodology, you create a daily, weekly, and monthly backup all at the same time. Then, as the month progresses, more and more backups are incorporated into the cycle. At any one time, you will have multiple backups of differing ages available. If you need to restore data, you can choose the most appropriate backup set, covering past days, weeks, months, or if you choose, even *years*.

The drawback to this approach is the number of backup media you must maintain. For six months worth of data, you will need six monthly tapes, four weekly tapes, and seven daily tapes — 17 tapes in all. Of course, you can always use even more daily or weekly tapes to enhance your protection level, but you should weigh your needs against the costs of maintaining a larger pool of tapes.

Integrity verification

One last word of advice — always verify the integrity of the backups created. We have heard of many incidents where an IT shop tried to recover data only to find out that the backups themselves were also damaged.

▶ Clustering

A, B, and C performing the work together, with A and B taking up the load if C goes down

Comparing Clustering and Redundancy

In clustering, your workload is shared by multiple system components or resources all operating at the same time. The separate and independent components act together as though they were a single resource.

Unlike redundancy, each component does its predetermined share of the workload — there is no "wasted" or redundant component that is not maximized.

In redundancy, each redundant component is designed to handle 100 percent of the workload, whereas in clustering, each component need only handle its equal share of the workload plus any additional workload depending on the desired tolerance to outages.

For example, if five components are configured for clustering, each component should at least be able to handle 20 percent of the workload. To compensate for *one* component going down, the remaining components should also be able to handle the additional 20% / 4, or five percent of the workload, for a total required capacity of 20 percent + 5 percent or 25 percent. If we design the system to handle *two* components failing at once, the 40 percent additional workload should be distributed to the remaining three components, for an additional workload of 40% / 3 or 13.3 percent, for a total required capacity per component of 33.3 percent.

As can be seen, clustering functions like redundancy, except that clustered components can be less powerful than redundant components, reducing the cost of deployment. To make the system more tolerant of outages, we can simply use more powerful components. If each clustered component is designed to handle the loss of *all* others, the required capacity would be 100 percent — full redundancy.

The key disadvantage of clustering is its relative complexity of implementing and configuring automatic workload sharing.

In theory, clustering allows for the addition of more components with the system designed to take advantage of the additional resource, easily and automatically sharing the workload. If users want better system performance, additional clustered components can be added, and performance will improve immediately.

Therefore, there are two major reasons for clustering: for scaling performance or for failover support. To scale performance, you configure clustering to divide the workload among additional, or more powerful, clustered components thereby increasing system throughput. To achieve failover support, your primary objective is to keep the system running despite the loss of one or two of the clustered components. Clustering enhances:

- **Reliability** — Because the workload is automatically transferred to the other components if one component goes down, the users experience no outage. At most, user might notice a degradation of performance.
- **Recoverability** — Since the load is automatically transferred to the operational components, the system recovers from the outage more seamlessly and more quickly.
- **Serviceability** — While the damaged component is being repaired, the system can still be functioning. Service work can then be done at any time, without a need to bring down the system.
- **Manageability** — The increase in number of components to manage and the relative complexity of the system configuration may at first make manageability of the system harder, but in the long term, the system is easier to manage since there are fewer outage-related emergencies.

Hardware and Software Clustering Examples

Hardware and software clustering is usually accomplished either by sharing data or disk storage devices, or by establishing completely separate components that share nothing. When data is shared, any of the systems in the cluster have access to the shared data or resources wherever they may be connected. In the "shared-nothing" approach, each system in the cluster owns a unique set of resources, with control over such resources delegated to another system if a failure occurs.

- **Failover clustering (Dell PowerEdge server example)** uses two connected PowerEdge servers configured to share external data storage devices. If one server fails, the other assumes the storage handled by the failed server, so users continue to have access to data. Additionally, the running server resumes the network services provided by the failed server, taking over the IP addresses of the failed server and restarting any applications that were running when the failure occurred. The two servers are interconnected via a Fast Ethernet network connection, and constantly monitor each other's health through a heartbeat mechanism. Either server can instantly react should a failure occur in the other. If a cluster-aware application is running on a server that has failed, another instance of that application can be started on the surviving server, allowing users to log back into the application and return to productivity.

- **Parallel computing** deploys clusters of independently functioning computer systems or processing units that may be configured to achieve both greater availability and higher levels of performance. This *clustering for scalability* approach uses as many clustered components as needed to achieve sufficient computing power. Since the workload is divided into smaller tasks that are processed by the clustered components working in parallel, large tasks can be completed faster than if they were executed by only one system. Failure of a single server in a scalable cluster has little impact on applications running on the server. From the user's perspective, the system is running uninterrupted with — at worst — a slight degradation in performance.

- **Dual Network Interface Cards (NICs)**, cited earlier as an example of redundancy, implement *Asymmetric* Port Aggregation. This allows two NICs to distribute outbound computer server traffic between them, providing greater bandwidth than a single NIC operating alone. The NICs act together to make it appear to the computer that there is only one device with only one network address. The two NICs can also implement *Symmetric* Port Aggregation, where two or more network connections combine into a higher bandwidth connection that can pass data in both directions. By combining several NICs, you can achieve gigabit speeds without replacing network hubs or switches.

- **Sun Cluster**, a product from Sun Microsystems, offers both failure protection and performance scaling for computer systems running on the Solaris operating environment. It allows the clustering of up to 256 processors and up to four nodes (instances of Solaris), with the capability to add or remove nodes while the entire cluster is on line. When a node goes down, other nodes in the cluster automatically takes over, picking up the "orphaned" workload. Sun Cluster also provides features such as local application restart, individual application failover, and local network adapter failover. The entire cluster can be managed as a single system, with an easy graphical user interface. Also, the nodes can be separated by up to 10 kilometers, so if a disaster befalls one node location, other nodes continue to operate.

IT Operations Clustering Examples

- **Multiskilled staffing** can be realized by training IT staff to perform tasks outside their normal work descriptions, so they can perform those tasks if the primary resource is not available.
- **Help desk operations** can be clustered by centralizing help desk functions, with multiple help desk personnel and locations answering the same help desk hotline and handling calls as they come in. The help desk hotline actually corresponds to several different phone numbers configured in a hunt group, so users only need to dial one number and the call automatically lands in any available line. This makes it easier to share the help desk workload — calls are routed to the next available help desk operator, whoever it is.

Environmental Clustering Examples

Multiple Internet service providers can be utilized, with traffic going to both connections at the same time. When one connection goes down, all transactions are handled by the single remaining link, although the users might experience some performance degradation.

Critical Success Factors

Automation and location are critical factors in clustering.

Automatic load-sharing

The system should be designed to automatically distribute the workload to every clustered component. As we have said, automation provides faster response to outages and is less prone to human error. Workload distribution is performed again whenever a component is added or removed from the clustered configuration.

Physical separation of clustered components

Clustered components should be located in different locations, to the extent that this can be done without introducing performance problems or adding unjustifiable cost. The goal: to minimize the chances that physical damage will impact more than one clustered component at the same time.

Fault Tolerance

Fault tolerance is a technique whereby systems or system components are designed to continue operating even during fault conditions. Some fault-tolerant systems are designed to withstand internal errors, whereas others address failures in external or connected components. Fault-tolerant systems are typically designed to address three types of errors:

- **Timing failures** — A service or the result of an operation does not take place within the expected period of time. For example, a network device may take too long to respond to an online status query.
- **Value failures** — The result of an operation is erroneous or outside of system parameters. For example, a computation results in an invalid number or out-of-range result.
- **Resource failures** — The use of a system resource is not possible or is outside of the accepted parameters (e.g., availability hours). For example, a system device is offline when it should be operational.

Note that most fault-tolerant systems can only tolerate error conditions temporarily. The IT organization must establish processes to ensure that corrective action can be taken before the fault tolerance capability is exceeded and the system fails.

Fault tolerance enhances:

- **Reliability** — The system is perceived to be more reliable since it continues operating despite problem conditions.

- **Recoverability** — Recovery from an outage is unnecessary if a system prevents the outage from occurring in the first place.
- **Serviceability** — During faulty conditions, a problem alert is generated as the system continues to function. This alert benefits the service team, which can schedule the system for maintenance when an outage will be less critical, for example, at night. The system becomes easier to service because the work can be planned and scheduled, and the problem can be adequately analyzed.
- **Manageability** — Fault tolerant systems that can continue to function under alert status are potentially easier to manage, since fault conditions can be carefully examined as they are occurring or while they are still present in the system.

Hardware Fault Tolerance Examples

- **Components that are sometimes used beyond their specifications** are strong candidates for fault tolerance. Many system components are designed to function within a given operating condition, such as temperature, load, or even hours of continuous use. Learn what the actual operating conditions will be, then choose system components that will function well beyond these values. For example, if computer room temperature is projected to be between 25–30 degrees Centigrade, use systems designed to operate well below 25 degrees and higher than 30 degrees. If air conditioning systems fail and cause room temperature to jump to 35 degrees Centigrade, there will be far less chance of equipment failure. Other examples include getting equipment that works with a wide range of electrical voltages, so abnormal power fluctuations can easily be handled.
- **RAID Level 5** is a hardware-level implementation of storage systems that provides fault tolerance. RAID-5 spreads data bits across multiple storage disks, adding check or parity bits for error recovery. When one disk in the array fails, the storage system can still accurately retrieve stored data.
- **Error Checking and Correcting (ECC) Memory** stores check bits that are generated by a special algorithm within the memory system itself. As each piece of data is retrieved, the algorithm

checks it against the code stored to validate it. With ECC memory systems, this algorithm not only detects bad data, it also identifies which bit is incorrect, and fixes the problem. ECC memory can only correct a limited number of erroneous bits. The limit depends on the specific algorithm that has been implemented.

- **Diskette Read/Write Retries** exploit diskette drive design, which provides some fault tolerance with respect to the diskette's magnetic media. When a read error is encountered, the drive automatically retries the operation a few times. In some cases, this retry is sufficient to retrieve the data from the weakening disk media. When these automatic retries are still not enough, the system asks the user whether it should retry some more, ignore the error, or abort the operation entirely.

Software Fault Tolerance Examples

- **The Log File Service of the Windows NT and Windows 2000 operating systems** can be set to log each storage disk input/output operation as a unique transaction, so when a user updates a file, the Log File Service logs redo (how to repeat it) and undo (how to roll it back) information for that transaction. If the update operation is successful, the file update is committed. Otherwise, the update is rolled back. This service is especially useful for ensuring successful data backup operations and when using error-prone storage media.

- **The Hot Fixing feature of Windows NT and Windows 2000** enables the system to handle write errors that occur because of a bad sector or area in a hard disk, by automatically assigning data to another sector or area without affecting running applications.

- **Bypassing of non-critical components** can be accomplished by software designed to continue providing essential functionality when non-critical components fail to load or are unavailable. For example, a well-designed word processor should load and work with documents even if selected fonts are unavailable, ideally warning the user of the issue.

Environmental Fault Tolerance Examples

- **Air conditioning capacity** should first be determined, then configured to operate at the lowest power settings. This will prolong the life of the air conditioning units themselves, and give them extra capacity for when external temperatures rise beyond normal limits.
- **Automatic Voltage Regulators (AVRs)** provide an easy, cost-effective way of ensuring stable power supplies when electricity sources fluctuate. Base your choice of an AVR on the amount of power fluctuations it can handle — the higher the range of protection, the better.

Critical Success Factors

Problem conditions are corrected as soon as possible — Fault-tolerant systems are only designed to provide temporary relief from the faulty condition. They buy you time to identify and resolve the cause of the problem. If the faulty condition is not corrected in time, the system may eventually fail to continue functioning properly. For example, AVRs will eventually be damaged if the fluctuating power source is not corrected or if the over-voltages get too high or too frequent.

▶ Isolation or Partitioning

A into B and C where a failure in B or C does not affect the other

With isolation or partitioning, a system is separated or divided into separate systems, so a fault condition in one does not affect the other. This technique is more effective in limiting the scope of outages than preventing them.

Isolation can be *physical* in nature — you split the system or component into two different physical components, and locate them separately. In other cases, only *logical* isolation is possible — you can ensure that a fault condition in one component does not propagate to another. Isolation enhances:

- **Reliability** — If system components are well isolated from each other, there is less risk of a system-wide outage.
- **Recoverability** — Since the fault condition causes an outage with a smaller scope, recovery is simpler, faster, and easier.
- **Serviceability** — You will need to bring down the entire system less often, and repair work can be done on a smaller subsystem. Servicing is easier since the subsystems are less complex, with fewer components to consider.
- **Manageability** — Smaller subsystems are easier to manage, and the tools required to manage them are often faster and less expensive. There is a tradeoff, however — the added complexity of coordinating the management activities of multiple subsystems.

Possible areas of isolation include:

- **Different corporate functions** — accounting system, sales system, etc.
- **Different locations** — regional, city, building, floors, room, etc.
- **Different purposes** — test system, development system, production system, demo systems, etc.
- **Different scope** — network, applications, databases, user terminals, etc.
- **Critical versus noncritical applications**
- **Public and internal facilities** — customer applications, back office applications, etc.

Hardware Isolation Examples

- **Separate servers** for applications or files can be installed in each department, instead of having a centralized server for the entire corporation. This allows most of the company to keep functioning even if a departmental server goes down, since fewer functions are affected. Departmental servers are usually cheaper to implement since processing workloads are far less than that of managing the entire corporation. Again, however, you now must manage multiple systems instead of one.

- **Production, test, and development systems** provide an opportunity to implement one of the most common and widely employed isolation techniques used by large computer installations. These installations use totally separate systems for designing applications (development systems), testing applications (test systems), and running applications (production systems). Programmers have greater freedom to design applications using the development system without worrying about affecting users. Using the test system, programmers can thoroughly test their new applications without impacting other users or programmers. Beta users of the new application can use this system, too. After sufficient testing, new applications can then be deployed in the production system with confidence.

- **Multinode networks** allow you to split your network into many subnetworks linked by bridges or routers. This approach not only has better fault isolation properties, but can also offer better performance. If one subnetwork begins to carry too much traffic, the other subnetworks are at least partially shielded. Carefully consider how you will subdivide your network. Leave networked devices in the same subnetwork if they usually communicate with each other. Otherwise, you will generate too much traffic between subnetworks. Many organizations create subnetworks based on the location of network devices (floor-by-floor) or by users' job functions.

Software Isolation Examples

- **Isolating data from applications** can be achieved by storing data in a different storage location from that of the applications. Since data changes more often than the application code, you can establish a different backup strategy for each. Also, damaged applications are less likely to corrupt data (especially with respect to virus-infected programs that can wreak havoc on storage media) if the applications are stored in different physical locations. Microsoft Access database applications, for example, can be split into a front-end database that contains the executable code (forms, queries, macros) and a back-end database that contains the data (tables). With table linking, the front-end database can link to the back-end database in another directory, drive, or even computer. This arrangement has another advantage — only the front-end databases must be distributed to users, and these are much smaller than equivalent databases including both code and data. Even more significant, data synchronization between multiple users is no longer a problem, because they are accessing the same back-end database.

- **Virtual Storage Architecture (IBM S/390 example)** isolates software processes from each other by using multiple, separate address spaces. Bad or faulty software that tries to access storage locations outside of its assigned address space is prevented from doing so.

- **Isolation by type of application** should be applied to maintenance and other utility applications. These should be run by a separate computer system from the one that executes user applications. For example, to the extent feasible, consider separating file/application services from systems management and administration.

- **Isolation by operating hours** can be used if you do not have the luxury of running maintenance tasks on a different computer from the one that runs user applications. With this approach, you can run maintenance tasks in off hours and run applications during normal office hours. As an example, all backup activities or systems diagnosis tasks (e.g., checking every file for computer viruses) can be done during a maintenance window when no user applications are allowed to run. Or you can configure the system to do these maintenance tasks immediately after the system is activated or before it is shut down.

Other Benefits of Isolation

Isolation has several additional benefits, as discussed next.

Minimize risk of changes

Problems that arise during the implementation of changes will have less impact if the systems are isolated from each other. Rather than applying the change to the entire system at once, implement it on one subsystem first, verify that the change is successful and has no ill effects, and then deploy it to all the other subsystems.

Reduce resource contention

With properly partitioned systems, users with high computing demands need not impact other users unnecessarily. For example, users of linear programming applications may be given their own high-performance system, separate from other users.

Maximize resources

You can focus resources on improving only the subsystems that require an upgrade. This can be much less expensive, and can also ensure that existing resources are fully utilized.

Simpler systems management procedures

It is often easier to design recovery, testing, repair, and other systems management procedures on a per subsystem basis. For example, it is much easier to define a backup methodology for a single PC than for a mainframe system. If the same PC configuration exists throughout the enterprise, you can replicate this design for every PC.

Systems management procedures become simpler for smaller subsystems since there are fewer system components to consider. Take note, though, that this does not necessarily simplify overall enterprise systems management. As we see in later chapters, if subsystems are not designed for manageability, enterprise systems management becomes very difficult, eliminating any initial benefits gained from isolation.

Critical Success Factors

- **Place a failure boundary between the system components** —
  When you implement partitioning, it is vital to establish a failure boundary between the two new subsystems, beyond which a failure in one subsystem cannot propagate. Determine how to minimize the systemwide impact of each probable failure, including these common failures:

- **Environmental failures** — fire, flooding, power outage, air temperature problem
- **Physical failures** — damage due to accidents, vandalism
- **Software failures** — hangs, illegal operations, viruses, Trojan horses, data corruption
- **People failures** — human error, hacking

Good partitioning can address each of these potential failures. For example, partitioning a server into two separate servers is optimal in the following situations:

- The servers are located in two separate rooms, floors, or buildings. This creates an *environmental* failure boundary — the walls between the rooms, the flooring between the floors, and/or the distance between the buildings.
- The servers are in two different computer casings, server racks, or cabinets. There is a *physical* failure boundary — the metal casing, or the shelves of the server rack, and/or the walls of the cabinets.
- The servers are running independent operating systems or in two separate networks. There is a *software* failure boundary — the operating system or network operating system.
- The servers are used by different sets of users — there is a *people* failure boundary.

- **Balance benefits of isolation versus impact to enterprise systems manageability** — Make sure that your partitioned subsystems will still be manageable after you split them. Do not sacrifice manageability in favor of the benefits of isolation with respect to cost savings and resource maximization. Remember that we are concerned with the *total* cost of ownership of the entire system.

    As an example, if you partition your mainframe system into many departmental servers, make sure that systems management tools are available for those departmental servers as well. In the mainframe environment, data backup is easy. With departmental servers, the cost of data backup is lower, but you might inadvertently use less reliable storage media, and make it more difficult to implement enterprise-wide data backup strategies. So make sure that your choice of subsystems is the right one.

As another example, if you are considering separating servers into multiple locations, reconsider your decision if security for these locations will be difficult to achieve. Outside of the traditional computer glass house, it can be a challenge simply to ensure that only authorized staff members touch the departmental servers and nobody accidentally trips over cables or flips the power switch.

▶ Automated Operations

Automated operations, or simply *automation*, is the technique of reducing or eliminating the need for human intervention for running the system. Its main objective is to replace manual procedures with tools or programs that can simulate or bypass the decision and the function normally performed by humans.

Automation is especially needed in today's computing environment because there is too much information to process manually, finding the right information is difficult, there are many resources to look after, and the interactions between these resources is complex. All these factors are conducive to human errors.

Human errors can take the form of:

- **Omissions** — Failing to do what should have been done. For example, a user failed to check his diskette for computer viruses prior to using it on the system, causing an infection of the entire hard disk.
- **Commissions** — Wrongly doing what should have been done. For example, a user accidentally uses the wrong backup tape, overwriting another department's data.
- **Decisions** — Choosing to do the wrong thing. For example, a user decides to shut down his computer while sharing a database application with other users, instead of contacting the database administrator. The result can be data corruption.
- **Performance** — Failing to do what should have been done *within certain performance parameters*, such as frequency,

speed, or accuracy. For example, a user might not change his workstation each month as agreed to, thereby exposing the system to security risks.

Automation enhances:

- **Reliability** — Outages due to human errors are eliminated. As help desk research shows, many calls are due to errors on the part of users, especially users of PCs (e.g., deleting program files, formatting the wrong diskette, etc.)
- **Recoverability** — System problem detection and recovery procedures can be done faster if automation tools are used. As an example, it would be virtually impossible to poll every device in a large enterprise network manually, and by the time a problem was detected, it would have led to an unacceptably long outage (or a call from frustrated users). Automated network monitoring tools can regularly query the device status of each network node, immediately raising an alarm (and even attempting to remotely reactivate the resource) if needed.
- **Serviceability** — Automation makes it easier to diagnose what might have gone wrong. Doubt and uncertainty are eliminated — everything that could have happened is either preprogrammed or stored in a system log somewhere, and not residing in some user's mind, subject to fears of management reprimand.
- **Manageability** — Managing the system becomes easier since you only need to set performance policies and procedures once and you are sure that the automated system will follow them. Automated systems have consistent quality of performance — they never get tired or bored doing the same thing repeatedly.

By monitoring, controlling, securing, or auditing computing resources, automation achieves the following:

- **Efficiency in detecting events and responding as needed** — An automated system can run around-the-clock doing the same thing repeatedly, never getting tired or careless. It eliminates the need to hire people for different work shifts doing repetitive tasks. If the task is highly repetitious but works within a given set of parameters where required responses are limited and can be known beforehand, you can probably automate it. Tasks that require creative problem solving or decision-making are best left to humans.

- **Thoroughness in obtaining data from all sources** — With automation, data gathering can be performed on all specified resources without fail. In fact, automated systems can work in the background while other system processes are performed, taking advantage of low processor or network bandwidth utilization times. Compare this with humans who can only do one task at a time perfectly well.
- **Accuracy in the performance of tasks** — Automated systems are set to perform a given set of tasks within given parameters, and they will do so for as long as the operating conditions are met. The risk of an automated system doing the wrong thing is very low.

Console and Network Operations Examples

- **Message routing and responses** can be effectively automated using tools that filter and route all system messages, instead of relying on system operators to read messages and identify the right recipients. Some system messages can even be routed to automated response software, which can act immediately without human intervention.
- **Environmental control** is an area where automation can easily play a role. Air conditioning systems can be electronic or computerized, activating automatically when a predefined temperature or humidity level is reached.
- **Customized commands, macros, and batch procedures** leverage the customizability of today's computer software, especially for PCs. Include programs that should be executed at every system boot in a Windows PC's Startup Folder or System Registry. These programs will then be run even if a system was accidentally rebooted without the user's knowledge.
- **Minimize keyboard input and user data entry wherever possible** — For example, create automatic systems for assigning filenames, instead of relying on the user's choice and risking him overwriting an existing file accidentally. If you must get input from the user, ask the user to choose from a predefined set of options, via a menu system. Wherever possible, avoid asking users to memorize command-line parameters.

Workload Management Examples

- **Start/stop operations** of applications, print jobs, and other system tasks can be automated based on predefined rules or conditions. A good example — scheduled runs of system utilities such as disk defragmenters and network resource status queries.
- **Load balancing and sharing** of systems maintenance and management tasks should be automated as much as possible. For example, in Windows 95/98, automate the deletion of temporary files when they reach a certain level, and utilize the automatic cache management function, which determines how much hard disk storage will be allotted to cache depending on available disk space and the number of programs running. Consider setting rules that determine which sets of users get the highest priority for resource allocation.
- **Startup parameters** can be included in a batch program that is automatically executed upon system or application activation. Also, alerts may be automatically generated before and during shutdown so users are aware of what is happening.

System Resource Monitoring Examples

- **Discovery and verification of resource configuration** is a prime candidate for automation. Otherwise, inventorying current system configurations, status, and features is a daunting task indeed. Today, many computers and other system resources automatically record their hardware and software configurations, making them available to specialized systems management software. Configuration management applications can interrogate these devices to build and update a database of system configuration data. PCs can provide information such as hard disk size and utilization, memory size, processor type, and many other parameters.
- **Polling for availability and resource usage statistics** is easily automated. Remote resources can be polled at given intervals rather than when an IT professional gets around to it, and the resulting data is more reliable and easier to analyze for trends. A simple example is the regular pinging of Internet resources.

Problem Management Applications

- **Detecting and reporting problems** is easily done if you already have a system in place that automatically checks for remote system resource status. When an unavailable resource is encountered, an alert can be issued to a problem management system in the form of a trouble ticket or a problem report. Also, monitoring software can maintain performance data and identify degraded performance, generating a warning. These applications typically allow you to specify your own performance thresholds.

- **Resolution of problems** can be done by systems with built-in automatic failure recovery features. For example, a network management application can automatically try to reset or reactivate a remote resource link that has gone offline, and generate an alert only if this recovery operation fails.

- **Recording system events** is an area in which automated logging facilities excel. They can capture all system events, including those that might otherwise be overlooked by a human. Not only are automated systems more thorough, they also are faster and more efficient at keeping records for later analysis. Logging need not be done by separate and expensive software. Many current systems have built-in logging facilities that simply need to be activated and utilized.

Distribution of Resources Example

Remote software distribution to remote computers lends itself to automation. When new software versions are rolled out, often all units must be updated as quickly as possible, especially if different versions of the software cannot be run reliably at the same time against the same data. Users also benefit if upgrades can be done outside regular office hours. Given the small windows of time acceptable to users, automating distribution becomes a necessity. Software distribution software allows this to occur even when the user is not around. It also allows a small number of IT staff members to upgrade thousands of systems concurrently.

Backup and Restore Examples

- **Hierarchical Storage Management (HSM)** systems automate the task of deciding which data to store in which backup storage medium. Backup of all data required by the enterprise is critical in a client-server environment where multiple databases reside on different computer servers. With HSM, the choice of which storage device to use can be based on the frequency of data updates, the age of the data, and how the data is used. Data that is constantly used is usually stored in faster (more expensive) storage medium (such as the user's hard disk or on a high-performance network server). Data accessed more rarely is stored in slower (and cheaper) storage media (such as tape drives, cartridge tapes, and laser disks). Especially sophisticated IT installations use robotic tape storage systems, so storing and retrieving tapes occurs without human intervention.
- **Off-peak hours backup** simply means utilizing automated backup software to schedule backup operations during off peak hours, or hours when the office is closed.

Human intervention in finding and loading off-line backups should be eliminated wherever possible. One solution is to use higher-capacity storage media such as optical disks or high-capacity tape drives, which can store many gigabytes of data on a single disk or tape. This minimizes the need to mount and dismount many tapes or disks to accommodate large amounts of data. If the use of these storage devices is not practical, consider automatic loading devices or robot librarians to handle finding, mounting, and dismounting backup media.

Critical Success Factors

- **Automate the right tasks** — Not all tasks can or should be automated. Humans should still handle tasks involving complex decision-making with hard-to-define rules. Automate operations that are:
  - **Highly repetitive** — These are typically tasks that must be performed at regular intervals — the more frequent the repetition, the more benefit you can achieve through automation.

- **Prone to human errors** — If experience has shown human operators are prone to error in performing a task, seek to automate that task.

- **Difficult to monitor** — Automate the performance of tasks whose execution is difficult to monitor.

- **Difficult to enforce** — Automate tasks that are often left undone intentionally by users or operators to save themselves time or effort, or for other personal reasons. For example, a good security practice is to change passwords regularly. You can use a security management system that automatically expires passwords at the appropriate interval, forcing users to change their passwords.

- **Automation tested prior to abandonment of manual procedures** — As with any well-planned project, test your automated system thoroughly before becoming fully dependent on it. Ideally, perform manual procedures alongside equivalent automated procedures for a period of time. Compare the results to ensure that the newly developed automated system produces the output you desire.

- **Document manual techniques for performing automated tasks** — Automated systems can break down. If this happens, clear documentation of manual alternatives allows you to continue performing essential operations while the automated systems are being restored. Remember that in a disaster mode, you will have to sacrifice some system tasks for the sake of network or processor bandwidth conservation — and automated systems management operations are likely to be set aside first.

- **Automation should not be easily bypassed without authority** — Make sure there is no easy way to change or stop the execution of automated systems by unauthorized individuals. This is especially important with respect to automated security management, change management, or performance management systems, where malicious users (inside or outside the company) may have an interest in making these systems run differently or not at all. For example, automatic password expiration systems, if halted, would simplify life for users who prefer not to remember new passwords — at the cost of corporate security.

- **Reduce barriers to automation** — Remove obstacles that can make automation difficult, expensive, or even impossible. These can include:
  - **Mechanical switching devices** — Old power switches, selectors, variable adjusters, and others make it virtually impossible to automate the tasks of switching on, selecting, and adjusting system resources. Fortunately, current equipment either employs mechanical switches with electronic bypass, or totally electronic switches that determine the state of the setting based on logical condition, not necessarily on physical position.
  - **Proprietary interfaces** — Interfaces are the means by which a device, program, or system exchanges information, acquires control instructions, or provides feedback to external devices, programs, and systems. Avoid proprietary interfaces that can become a barrier to automation in the future. If you ensure that your software systems conform to management infrastructure standards such as DMI or SNMP, you can easily implement automation tools that support change management, network management, configuration management, and other management disciplines.
- **Input/output involving removable physical media** — Removable media makes automation challenging, because it is usually physically separate from the device that uses it. For example, storage tapes, such as cartridges or AIT tapes, are typically organized into a tape rack and kept in a vault for protection. How do you automate the loading and unloading of this storage media? Impossible, unless you use an expensive robot or tape librarian system. As mentioned earlier, one alternative is to use online storage as much as possible, depending on large capacity hard disk arrays or even optical disk jukeboxes.

▸ Access Security Mechanisms

Every high-availability system needs to incorporate measures that limit access to, or exposure of, sensitive resources. These measures are directed towards eliminating damage caused by humans, whether intentional or accidental. Security mechanisms enhance:

- **Reliability** — Unauthorized actions are controlled, reducing the frequency of possible outages.

- **Recoverability** — Scope of outage is limited to breached areas only, so recovery is simpler.

- **Serviceability** — If all activities during a security breach are recorded, it's easier to identify the steps needed to fix damage.

- **Manageability** — Greater control over resources, their configuration and utilization results in more effective management of the system overall.

Steps to Secure Access

Some IT professionals have the mistaken notion that securing access simply involves restricting access. In reality, several steps must be taken.

Step 1: Identify the person requesting access

In this step, you identify the person requesting access to a sensitive resource. You can do this simply by requesting some form of identification, which can take one of the following forms:

- **For physical entry of a person** — identification card, statement of name, etc.

- **For entry of a user into a secured application** — user ID, login name, etc.

- **Other identifiers** — such as email addresses and credit card numbers

These identification methods give you a higher level of trust towards an unknown individual, based on your knowledge of how identification cards should look, who is a valid employee, which user IDs, login names, and email addresses are acceptable, and the valid range of credit card numbers. In certain situations where only a basic level of security is needed, this may be sufficient. Since you will depend on these identification resources, they should be kept confidential from the outside world.

Step 2: Verify the identity

When a higher level of security is needed, make sure the person is not impersonating someone else. Verification can be achieved in several ways, depending on the scenario:

- **For physical entry of the person** — by checking the photo on the identification card, asking the purpose of entry, double-checking with the destination, and similar techniques.
- **For entry of a user to a secured system** — by checking for a password, through biometrics (the use of physical characteristics of the user to validate an identity, such as fingerprint or retinal image), by checking validity of electronic signature, and other sophisticated techniques.
- **For others** — requiring the person to answer questions only the real person would know the answer to (e.g., mother's maiden name, name of favorite pet, and the like).

Most secured systems give people access if they successfully complete this step. Since much is at stake, high levels of security should be afforded to lists of passwords, employee bio-data, and other information used for identity verification.

Step 3: Control access

For applications requiring even greater security, also limit the activities an individual is able to perform even after you have given them access to a secured area or system. Here are several approaches:

- **For physical entry of the person** — by requiring the person to wear a badge that visibly identifies where he is permitted to go, by asking someone from inside to escort him at all times, or by requiring him to leave the secured area by a certain time.
- **For users requiring access to a secured system** — by disabling facilities or functions he should not use (e.g., copying, deleting, modifying, etc.), by limiting access to specified databases and resources, or other constraints.
- **For others** — by placing firewalls between secured systems and public, untrusted systems. These firewalls filter all incoming and outgoing communications traffic based on acceptable source, destination, contents, and function.

Step 4: Monitor all activities

You can achieve even higher levels of security by having a person or automated system monitor and respond in real time to the activities of people working in secured systems. This is an expensive solution normally reserved for high security applications. Monitoring can be done in the following ways:

- **For physical entry of the person** — by video monitoring, recording in/out of people through secured doorways, roving security staff members, and other techniques.

- **For users requiring access into secured applications** — by recording actions and examining system activity logs, by reviewing application audit trails, and through the use of security monitoring software.

Types of Security

The key to effective security implementation is to balance your implementation of security measures. Start by implementing security perimeters, whereby you control physical and logical access to sensitive resources by area. First, secure the largest area within your control, working your way towards the resources to be protected. If you can eliminate the security threat as far away from the sensitive resource as possible, your risks are minimized. Let's look at some examples.

Physical security

Start by securing the building facility, then the floor where the sensitive assets are located, then the entrance to the office space, then the entrance to the room where the assets are located, and finally the storage space where it is kept.

For example, to physically secure the company Internet server, you can start by requiring all visitors to present an identification card at the building front lobby. The lobby attendant may choose to verify the purpose and validity of the visitor. You can also set policies regarding days and times visitors are allowed, types of acceptable identification cards, and what visitors can bring into the facility.

At the floor where the Internet server is located, you could have a main entrance between the elevator and the office, for instance, a door that is normally closed. You could equip the door with a magnetic card access mechanism. In this scenario, the ID cards of legitimate entrants have a magnetic security stripe that enables their access. Visitors seeking entry knock or ring a bell to get someone inside to open the door for them. At this point, the person opening the door can check on the visitor's destination and purpose. There should be only one main entrance per floor, with all other doors designed to open only from the inside.

In the office area, you might place all computing equipment, including the Internet server, inside an enclosed area commonly known as a "glass house." Naturally, entry into this secured area would require the access card of the system administrator or anybody else with the authority to handle the equipment inside.

Inside the glass house, if possible, protect power and communication cables from accidents by using raised flooring and running all cables underneath. Doing so prevents people from tripping over cables and causing system outages, and also organizes the cabling, making it easier to maintain.

The Internet server should ideally be installed in a computer rack that is locked at all times, with the key kept by the system administrator or the computer operations supervisor. We all know how easy it is to turn off a computer by simply pushing a button or flipping a switch. Placing the computer in a rack can prevent this from happening. Bolt the rack to the floor to prevent unnecessary movement.

You should also implement some form of protection from natural and man-made calamities such as floods and fires. The use of monitoring cameras may also be appropriate.

The computer server itself should have some form of locking mechanism on its casing to prevent tampering. Consider replacing standard screws with screws that require unusual tools. Remember, also, to secure all cables in place.

Network security

Implement network security by first addressing elements of your network that are accessible via the Internet, a public, untrusted network. Next, address your company's internal wide area network. Then, address each local area network.

For example, to secure the company Internet server that is accessible via the public Internet, start by keeping company domain names and IP addresses confidential. Discourage employees from using their company email addresses when registering for services in the public Internet (e.g., mailing lists). This can be part of a broader corporate email security policy along the following lines — all email using company email addresses (under the company domain) is corporate property, and management reserves the right to read any email as it deems necessary. You might encourage users to register for a free email account (e.g., Hotmail) for their own private use.

Between the public and the company internal network, install a firewall to police the traffic between the two networks. Using this firewall, you can block specific traffic by destination, source, or type of transaction.

If your system uses the public telephone system as part of the network extension for connecting remote users or devices, then you should keep these modem dial-up telephone numbers private to minimize break-in attempts.

For point-to-point modem connections, use encryption between the two points, and implement dial-back verification whenever a remote connection is initiated (e.g., the modem knows that it is only supposed to get a call from a specific telephone number, so every time a connection is initiated, the modem hangs up the phone and calls that number to establish the connection). If an unauthorized individual is attempting to connect via one of your dial-up ports, he will not get the callback since he is using a number that has not been preauthorized.

At the wide area network level, utilize security-monitoring software that checks for illegal transactions, or encrypt traffic between different sites.

At the local area network level, strictly enforce the use of login names and passwords. Each workstation should have screen savers that automatically lock the computer during inactive periods so the user need not log in and out repeatedly. Finally, ensure that network server configuration files are kept private to the system administrator.

Application security

Start securing applications at the session level, next at the user level, then at the data access level, and finally, at the activity level.

At the session level, consider limiting execution of applications to certain times of day, with each session lasting only for a specified duration. Also consider limiting the number of concurrent sessions running on the same machine, or even automatically ending sessions if there is no input from the user for a specified time. Sessions can also be restricted to execute from specified workstations only (e.g., accounting applications can only be executed from workstation addresses belonging to the accounting department).

At the user level, the application should only allow execution by previously specified users, with each user providing a password. Every user login should be recorded for audit. All passwords should adhere to password guidelines we discuss in the next section. All logins should be limited to three attempts, and if these are exceeded, login names should be locked out until the administrator reactivates them. Finally, it is crucial to update your user lists whenever employees leave the company, voluntarily or otherwise.

At the data access level, you can restrict access to certain databases depending on the user. Monitor and track changes to databases. Prevent users from accessing directory or database structure, so they cannot get information they are not supposed to have. Hide sensitive directories or files, or protect them with passwords.

At the activity level, certain users should be allowed to do reads only, while others are given write or update capability. All activities should be recorded for future security audit or review. When possible, use secure communication protocols like Secure-HTTP for sensitive transactions.

Computer resource security

First, review your options for securing applications. Next, address software utilities, then operating systems, and finally, BIOS security.

- **Program level** — Every application should have a user identification and verification facility to restrict access. Programs should be prevented from executing commands that bypass operating system functions and directly call on system BIOS commands.
- **Software utilities level** — Remove or disable software utilities or functions your users do not need, because of their potential negative impact on the stability or integrity of the overall system. In

DOS and Windows systems, for example, remove FDISK (for low-level formatting of hard disks) and FORMAT (for completely erasing and preparing a hard disk). You'll sleep more peacefully knowing that users cannot inadvertently delete their entire drives.

Establish a company policy against users installing their own software utilities, especially those from unverifiable sources (e.g., Internet shareware downloads). This not only prevents the introduction of unnecessary complexity to user systems, it also eliminates a backdoor by which computer viruses can enter.

Take proactive steps, including installing software to enhance security, such as antivirus software, encryption and decryption programs, and file deletion utilities.

- **Operating system level** — Begin by taking advantage of your computer's security features and functions. For example, hide system files from normal system commands, so you can prevent their accidental deletion or change. With DOS, changing the file type to Archive or System accomplishes this. With Windows 95/98/2000, you can set Windows Explorer to hide certain file types. If the operating system has file-level access control, use it properly. Change all default system passwords as soon as you install the system — these default passwords are, of course, public knowledge.

- **Computer BIOS level** — The BIOS is the program that runs right after the computer is powered on, and just before the operating system starts loading. To ensure BIOS security, first set a system supervisor password, to prevent unauthorized changes that could render a system inoperable. If your PC has a BIOS feature that prevents programs from writing to the hard disk boot sector, thereby preventing boot-sector virus infection, activate this feature.

Also disable system boot-up using removable storage media such as diskettes. Ideally, boot the computer from the network, which is likely to be more secure. Some organizations remove diskette drives from workstations, eliminating the transfer of files into or out of the computer.

Password Management

As already mentioned, passwords represent a key opportunity for verifying user identity. To effectively use passwords for security, however, you must implement an effective password management discipline. Keep in mind the challenge that your users face. So many systems require logins and passwords nowadays, users are forced to memorize login names and passwords left-and-right. They resort to shortcuts that compromise security, such as:

- **Using the same password for all logins** — This practice is more convenient for the user, but the impact of a lost or compromised password becomes disastrous.

- **Using trivial, easy-to-remember passwords,** such as pet names, common words, and even variants on the user's own name. Of course, if a password is easy for a user to remember, it's usually easy for a determined intruder to guess.

- **Writing down passwords** — Ill-intentioned people can find the written passwords, which are often kept in plain sight.

Here are some steps towards quality password management.

Step 1: Enforce password selection guidelines

Educate users on the proper kinds of passwords, and consider using password management software that can enforce your restrictions. Quality passwords should have these characteristics:

- Minimum of eight characters so there are many possible combinations

- Include at least two numbers for added complexity

- Must not be similar to previous passwords used, at least three generations back

- Must not refer to system resources (e.g., syspac, admin)

- User-related information should be avoided (e.g., girlfriend's name, pet's name, middle name)

- Must not be common names of people, places, or things (e.g., america, paper)
- If possible, let security system assign randomly generated passwords (e.g., 1byrk9ps)

Step 2: Expire passwords regularly

Depending on the sensitivity of the asset being secured, expire user passwords quarterly, monthly, weekly, or even daily, asking users to provide new passwords so any compromised passwords immediately become obsolete.

Step 3: Expire assigned passwords on first use

Security administrators should assign initial passwords prior to activating a new user. (These should *not* be the default passwords set by software or hardware manufacturers.) The first time the new user logs in, he should immediately be asked to provide a new password.

Step 4: Disable user accounts after successive invalid password attempts

Login attempts should be limited, to foil those who seek to compromise system security by trying out many different passwords. For very sensitive applications, allow no more than three successive invalid attempts. Beyond three attempts, the user ID should either be:

- **Temporarily disabled** — Requires the system administrator to manually reactivate the user ID. (However, never automatically disable the system administrator's account after successive invalid attempts — you may not have a way to restore that ID without a full system reinstall. Check your system documentation.)
- **Temporarily disabled until a certain amount of time elapses** — This approach may not be foolproof against hackers, but it can make their task much more time consuming.
- **Temporarily inaccessible from the workstation where the invalid logins were attempted** — Reset the counter of password input attempts after a user logs in successfully, as normal users can

make honest mistakes in typing their passwords. If possible, display the invalid password input of the user if it is incorrect. This information makes it easier for the honest user to find his mistake. For example, the user might inadvertently have left the CAPS-Lock key active while typing a case-sensitive password.

Step 5: Educate users on how to protect their password information

No matter how good your system security program is, if the user fails to safeguard his password, sensitive assets can easily be compromised. Users should be aware of what sensitive assets are, how the assets are threatened, and why their access must be password protected. Offer suggestions on protecting password information. At the least, password lists should not reside in users' computer. If passwords are stored in computer files, the files should be encrypted and protected by a master password the user has not written down anywhere. If passwords are stored in other electronic devices such as PDAs or electronic organizers, these too should be password protected. If the user must write down password information, it should be kept in an envelope and stored under lock and key. Finally, if a user suspects his password has been compromised, encourage him to report the incident to the system security administrator immediately, so all his passwords can be reset.

Critical Success Factors

- **Top-down enforcement of security policies** — Security management should be a directive from the highest levels of management. This gives it the importance and attention that it deserves. Protecting corporate security should be a condition of employment that all employees agree to.

- **Regular user security awareness programs** — Security is an ongoing requirement. It is normal for people to wane in observing security practices occasionally. Regular "refresher" programs on good security practices are needed in every company, large or small. Schedule different activities throughout the year to ensure a campaign that is effective year-round. For example, you might hold an annual security seminar and require every employee to attend. You might require employees to pass a security practices exam each year. Individual employees could be required to sign a security responsibilities contract each year. You might regularly send out security alert memos or emails, publish quarterly security newsletters, and post security-related posters.

- **Thorough identification and protection of all system backdoors** — You must become aware of all possible means of access to your information system. This requires in-depth knowledge of the inner workings of your systems and applications, which is not always easy to acquire. Fortunately, numerous organizations provide access to security alerts, software bugs information, and other materials pertaining to security administration.

  When it comes to physical security, don't forget to secure all access paths to your sensitive information systems. The main door to many computer rooms is secured, but the fire exit may not be. (Of course, the fire exit must remain unlocked, but you might allow it to open only from the inside, not from the fire exit staircase.) Doors, windows, air ducts, and other possible passageways should all be considered.

- **Testing and auditing of access control mechanisms** — Don't wait for an outsider with malicious intent to show you that your access control mechanism no longer works. You should periodically test your protection systems unannounced, possibly by pretending to gain unauthorized access. Try logging in as a user and guessing passwords, performing an invalid access attempt, or hiring an outsider to attempt to gain access to the computer room by using fake IDs, or by lying their way in — often called "social engineering." You can even hire "tiger teams" of authorized hackers who will attempt to penetrate your secured systems for a fee, and then provide advice on enhancing security.

- **Updating of security tools as often as needed** — Today's security protection is easily made obsolete by newer technology falling into the hands of those who want to use it for illicit purposes. Antivirus tools must be updated at least on a weekly basis to account for new computer viruses. Encryption software needs to be updated with longer encryption keys, as the computing power for cracking shorter ones becomes more widely accessible. And security software needs to be enhanced to take into account new systems or applications that must be protected.

▶ Standardization

Setting specifications for the hardware, software, procedures and techniques that will be used throughout your IT infrastructure is known as standardization. This discipline is often disregarded in favor of giving users freedom to choose their own sets of applications or interfaces to the corporate system. However, unbridled freedom often leads to chaos and problems with system manageability. IT managers should think twice about giving users too much flexibility, and instead mandate system-wide standards. Doing so enhances:

- **Reliability** — The system has fewer types of components to manage so is less complex and easier to integrate. This leads to better overall system performance, greater predictability, and fewer problems.
- **Recoverability** — Since fewer types of components must be considered, it is easier to develop recovery procedures for the entire system.
- **Serviceability** — Less work is required to master your equipment, since you have fewer components to become expert with. Since you now have time to achieve deeper expertise in the components you've standardized upon, you reduce the risk of unintentionally introducing more problems during the repair process.
- **Manageability** — It is easier to manage system inventory, since you have fewer suppliers and types of equipment to manage.

Several other important benefits can be derived from standardization:

- **Consistency of operations** — When there are only a few types of systems or applications, you need fewer operating procedures.
- **Better resource utilization** — Your information systems resources are better utilized, since you don't need to support duplicate software packages accomplishing the same function. Also, your people invest less time in exchanging and converting data amongst different systems. For example, if your users utilize both Microsoft Word and Lotus Ami Pro for word processing, whenever Word users share files with Ami Pro users, they must first convert the document's format before getting down to work.

- **Easier training** — Obviously, the fewer applications you must train users on, the smaller investment you must make in creating training manuals, developing courses, and conducting training sessions.

- **Fewer IT skills required** — Reduced system complexity means your IT personnel need fewer skills to support their users. Your help desk needs fewer product specialists, and they can focus on deepening their expertise in remaining system components.

- **Simpler backup and recovery scenarios** — Having fewer system components makes it easier to plan for disaster recovery, because you have fewer scenarios and combinations of events to plan for.

Hardware Standardization Examples

- **Standard computing platform** — Perhaps the easiest and broadest standard you can implement is that of an enterprise-wide computing platform. Will your system be mainframe-based, AS/400-centric, UNIX server based, or PC-centric? Which applications will reside on which platforms? Whatever your choices are, we recommend having no more than three strategic platforms.

- **Standard storage capacity** — Set a minimum amount of storage and memory for all PCs you deploy, so you can count on the availability of this much storage and memory when you develop and deploy new applications. Obviously, you will need to update your standard occasionally to keep pace with changing requirements. If possible, upgrade all systems at once, enterprise-wide.

- **Standard warranty coverage** — Purchase products from vendors who offer attractive standard warranty periods and service arrangements. If possible, specify three-year warranty coverage, and have warranty work done on site. Do not settle for carry-in repair service. If you can standardize on warranty arrangements, you won't have to recall which equipment qualifies for each level of service when an outage strikes.

- **Standard vendor** — Purchase equipment from one vendor, or a few carefully selected vendors. This simplifies support and helps you avoid finger pointing, especially for complex problems involving multiple hardware components. In our experience, this finger pointing is a key reason outages are unnecessarily prolonged.

- **Standard environmental requirements** — Simply put, ensure that the equipment you plan to use together can work in the same location. Consider operating voltage and other electrical requirements, as well as temperature and humidity specifications.

Software Standardization Examples

- **Standard operating system** — Standardize on as few operating systems as possible. This simplifies support and avoids the need to purchase different versions of the same software for different operating systems. Make sure your choice of operating system will be acceptable to end users. We've seen a company try to enforce an old and unpopular operating system simply because it was their own product. Little by little, users installed bootleg copies of another operating system, until the users lost faith in the IT organization and decided to outsource.

- **Standard set of applications** — Select a standard office suite, graphics software, and other off-the-shelf programs. If possible, use an enterprise-wide software infrastructure for core business applications instead of gluing together many different applications that were never intended to be integrated. Enterprise-wide data integration is a key reason SAP and similar suites are widely used in large and medium-scale enterprises.

- **Standard application interfaces** — If you must design your own applications, standardize the user interface. You could have a standard menu system that uses common menu layout and terminology. For example, to open a stored file, you could use File Open in all your applications, instead of some having File Read, or Disk Open, or Data Access, etc. We recommend using a menu system your users are already familiar with, say, that used by most Microsoft Windows applications. Windows and most other contemporary operating environments have official standards guides programmers can use to standardize interfaces drawing upon industry best practices.

Network Standardization Examples

- **Standard protocol** — Standardizing on a single network protocol has obvious advantages for network performance, compatibility, and manageability. Today, the network protocol of choice is TCP/IP, the protocol used by the Internet.

- **Standard technology** — In the long run, your network will be more stable if you standardize on only a few networking technologies. Choose a base technology your major network components will operate on, and use newer technologies only on areas of your network where the added features or speed is a must.

- **Standard supplier** — Incompatibilities between different vendors' networking components can lead to degraded network performance that is difficult to detect, identify, and correct. Getting as many components from the same supplier gives you greater confidence they will work together well. Naturally, your choice of supplier should depend on product breadth, track record, and conformance to industry standards.

Processes and Procedures Standardization Examples

- **Standard systems management procedures** — Since systems management should be treated as an enterprise-wide discipline, the same sets of procedures should be followed across every function and department, with few exceptions. For example, problem reporting should always be done via the corporate help desk. Even top managers should be required to call the help desk, not place calls directly to the IT management.

- **Standard reporting guidelines** — The format, terminology, content, and frequency of reports should be agreed upon throughout the enterprise.

Naming Standardization Examples

- **Standard user names** — Should user login names include a surname, or specify job function (auditor, CFO, techsup)? Using job functions may simplify administration of usernames as employee changes occur. Should email addresses be personalized, or should you use a coding scheme that preserves each individual's anonymity, especially for mail addresses utilized in public communications? Some companies use the job function as the email address (e.g., notebook_sales@computervendor.com), so customers can always reach the function they need, regardless of who is actually assigned to that position. Whatever choice you make, standardize on it throughout the organization.

- **Standard data resource names** — For data that is created by users and shared with other users, establish a naming convention that can be easily understood by all potential users. If you do, users can recognize the likely content of a file by looking at its name. It is frustrating to see filenames such as Harry.wrd, Myplan.xls, or Project-update.123. With today's PCs capable of handling long file names, why not use filenames such as — Mgmt-meeting-04-99.doc, Security-plan.xls, or Disaster-recovery-plan-version2.123.

- **Standard data directory structure** — It can be frustrating for users to find important files on other users' computers. Establish a standard directory structure for every end user computer. This directory structure could follow the way the different departments are organized and the purpose of the files contained in the subdirectories. For example:

Company files:
Sales — Proposals | Templates | Strategies | Plans
Personnel — Forms | Letters | Evaluations | Reports
IT — Procedures | Reports | Performance Data

Every employee need not have all subdirectories in his computer — only the ones in which he needs to store files. At the corporate level, you could keep a centralized copy of all user files, and if all users follow this standard directory structure, it will be relatively easy to group their files together. A standardized directory system also makes it easier to centralize the backup of individual PCs across the network, because you can easily identify which folders or directories contain business data.

- **Standard computer resource names** — Every enterprise information resource should be named according to a standard naming convention. Workstation and network component names, for example, could have the department location+asset type+asset count (e.g., MktgPC001, MisSvr01, EastOpsHub01). Storage disks could be named according to the data that they contain (e.g., Syspack01, ProdData01, Test02). Include everything that needs to be labeled, including cables, removable storage media, and computer peripherals. With a system like this in place, management is simplified, and there is less risk of trouble due to misidentified system components.

- **Standard approach to naming** — Standardize the minimum and maximum length of names (e.g., user IDs should be at least eight characters long); the language to use (e.g., English); and acceptable abbreviations (e.g., Acctg for accounting, and not Acct, Actg, or Accountg). If there are special symbol characters your systems need to avoid, specify this in your standard. We recommend that every organization have some form of corporate dictionary that explains the standard naming conventions and common terminology used.

Critical Success Factors

- **Gain the support of top management** — It can be difficult gaining organization-wide acceptance for standardization. Senior management must be leading advocates. Otherwise, some users will do everything they can to resist change, especially if the change involves junking their favorite program or long-time habits.

- **Enforce standards sooner rather than later** — It is easier to implement something new when the users have no previous experience with an alternative way of doing things. Establish new standards when you roll out new applications, systems, or processes. Don't make the mistake of letting the users make their own decisions and then choosing a standard based on what is dominant — you will always create dissatisfied users this way. Carefully analyze user requirements analysis first, so you can choose a standard your users will accept.

- **Choose standards that are acceptable to most users** — Remember that IT's purpose is to support users' computing needs. If you choose a standard users dislike, you probably did a poor job of determining their needs. If the popular choice will be overly expensive or difficult to manage, you must weigh the benefits and costs carefully, from the perspective of the overall enterprise.

- **Reevaluate your standards regularly** — Technology and user needs change rapidly. When the standards you use are no longer at par with the current technologies, when your competitors are running their business better than you are by using newer technologies, or when your technology is failing in the marketplace, you may need to update your standards. When users start clamoring to use a new standard, begin installing and using new systems without your knowledge, and report dwindling satisfaction with your service, your standards may no longer be serving their needs.

- **If possible, conform to industry de facto standards** — When deciding on corporate standards, get ideas from the industry. What systems are in use by most other companies? What technology do the most suppliers support? What procedures and skills are taught to most IT professionals? Even for IT operations and procedures, you can consult professional organizations that specialize in this area. For example, consider the IT management procedures advocated by the ITSMF (i.e., Information Technology Systems Management Forum). When professional certifications exist for certain skills, you can be sure that those skills address technologies that are dominant in the industry (e.g., Microsoft Certified Professional).

- **Be leading edge, not bleeding edge** — Only avoid industry standards when a newer alternative offers a truly compelling competitive advantage.

- **Make room for future user requirements** — When deciding on a standard, make sure that near-term user requirement changes are taken into consideration. This will prevent you from constantly redefining your standard, and confusing both your IT organization and your users. For example, when standardizing on the amount of computer memory to be installed in every user's workstation, determine first if there will soon be major changes in user applications that will require more memory, or if your company is forecasting a major increase in volumes that will increase the number of computer transactions and necessitate the use of faster programs. Don't just consider purchase cost constraints when setting your standards — you might end up spending more when an upgrade is required. Also consider labor costs, lost business opportunities, and the overall impact on your systems.

Transitioning to Standardization

Standardization is a sensitive political issue in most organizations, especially when it comes to user PCs and applications. Many users want the same software that they use at home or where they used to work, since this is what they are most familiar with. The popular choice may sometimes be unfavorable from the business standpoint. What do you do?

As with any standards program, the IT organization can transition the users towards new standards, and implement measures that can subtly force users to accept them:

- **Sell the merits of using the standard** — You have to "sell" standards to users. You can do so by conducting seminars, publishing newsletters, or sending out mailers that discuss the advantages of using the new standards. This selling should be continual — before, during, and after rollout. Gain senior management buy-in early in the process, so senior managers can become your allies during migration. Emphasize advantages from the user's point of view. Cite third-party support for the standards you've chosen, and tell users they will learn skills that are in demand even outside the company.

- **Make the non-standard alternative more difficult to get** — You may still allow non-standard components in your system if a user vehemently insists, but you can make it more difficult for users to get them. You can lengthen the approval, procurement, and installation process for non-standard components, require more signatures, add more rigid acceptance testing, or lower the priority of non-standard installations.

- **Make the non-standard difficult to use** — Because of resource constraints, limit support to standardized hardware and software components. If users wish to use non-standard components, they must get their own training and ongoing support. If the non-standard component introduces problems, the user will be fully responsible for the extra cost of resolution. One company established the following support policy for non-standard PC configurations: "If there is anything wrong with your computer and we see that it does not contain the standard set of software we initially installed, we will only proceed with problem diagnosis and repair if we can restore the standard set of applications first." This policy certainly deterred people from downloading and installing their own software — except for a few adventurous users who had extensive knowledge of PCs.

▶ Summary

Several techniques for information systems design and implementation can significantly improve the key elements of higher availability, recoverability, serviceability, reliability, and manageability. These techniques are:

- Redundancy
- Fault tolerance
- Backup
- Clustering
- Partitioning
- Automated operations
- Access security mechanisms
- Standardization

In many cases, these techniques are already implemented in today's products, especially those made by reputable vendors. It is only a matter of knowing how they have been incorporated, and how you can apply them in your specific environment. The Appendix of this book contains detailed information on how some of these availability techniques are implemented in many common products. You can use this information to jumpstart your efforts to maximize availability in your IT environment.

Special Techniques for System Reliability

▶ The Use of Reliable Components

The first technique that specifically targets reliability is obvious — the use of reliable components. What is not so obvious is how to choose components that are reliable. This chapter provides recommendations about maximizing the reliability of every system component — not just hardware and software, but also personnel, suppliers, and the information technology environment.

Techniques for Maximizing Hardware Component Reliability

In the following sections, we cover techniques for maximizing the reliability of your system's hardware components.

Choose components with low failure rates

By failure rate, we mean the average rate at which a component fails. According to experts, the failure rate is usually high early in the life of a product. This stage of a product's life might correspond to the first few days the product is used, or the first release of newly developed software, or the first version of new hardware with unproven firmware. After these early problems, failure rates typically decrease, and then remain constant as most products age or mature. Eventually, of course, failure rates again rise. Products may become worn out; or compatibility problems may arise as newer systems are introduced; or hardware may be overwhelmed by user demands that increase beyond its original specifications.

Choose components that have high MTBF

Often, the specifications of components produced by reputable manufacturers contain an estimate of reliability expressed in terms of MTBF or Mean Time Between Failures. MTBF typically means units of component time per failure (e.g., machine-hours per failure). MTBF is estimated by dividing the total operating time accumulated by a group of components within a given time period, by the total number of failures in that time period.

An MTBF of 100,000 hours means that one component running for 100,000 hours can expect to encounter one failure. Two similar components running for 100,000 hours can expect to encounter one failure apiece, or two total failures. In other words, if you install two components, you can expect one failure every 50,000 hours. If you install 100 of these devices, you can expect 100 failures in 100,000 hours, or one failure every 1,000 hours.

MTBF is *not* equal to a component's lifetime. However, it does give you a rough idea of how many backup components you'll need in place to protect against potential failures. Let's continue with the example above: 100 devices with an MTBF of 100,000 hours. If you plan to operate all 100 devices 10 hours a day, 7 days a week — or 3,360 hours a year — you can calculate expected failures as follows:

1 failure per 1,000 hrs × 3,360 hrs = 3.36 failures per year

From this, you might decide to purchase three or four spares.

Remember that MTBF is an *average*. You may experience better or worse results in individual devices, but if you deploy a large number of similar devices, your overall experience should be similar to the vendor's specifications.

Purchase from reputable suppliers

Purchase hardware only from companies with a proven track record of quality. This may cost more, but in the long run the additional expense will be worth it. Don't take the vendor's word for it, either — look for vendors that have received independent product awards for reliability and quality. Check references. Read the product's warranty terms and conditions closely, and look for a longer warranty — it means a vendor is willing to bet on the product's reliability.

Use technical specifications as a gauge

If a product has a wider range of operating conditions, it's less likely to experience problems when operated in normal conditions, because its components will not be as heavily stressed. For example, choose PCs with a wider temperature operating range, LAN cards with higher maximum speeds, and cables with smaller signal losses or greater maximum distances. Some equipment, especially equipment intended for military or industrial use, is designed from the ground up to function in more severe conditions. If you use this equipment in normal office environments, it's far less likely to break down.

Choose products with fewer parts or greater integration

Fewer parts mean fewer internal conflicts and less risk of failure. Fewer mechanical parts can also mean less friction, a main cause of wear and tear in most mechanisms.

Avoid newly developed products whenever possible

We all know that the controlled environment in which products are developed is very different from the normal office environment in which we work. Given this fact, it is wise not to buy models that are "fresh from the development lab." It is better to wait until the product has gone through a fair amount of field-testing in office environments at the hands of real users. It is here that the product endures the "abuse" of users and is exposed to factors that can never be completely simulated in the development lab. After some time, get feedback from users who have actually used said product before you make that purchasing decision. Better still, wait for the revised or upgraded model.

Follow maintenance schedules diligently

We cannot overemphasize the importance of diligently following your vendor's recommended maintenance schedules. People often defer parts replacement when they see that the part itself seems to be in good condition. But if you really want high reliability, why risk it? A part by itself may look good, but it could already have a negative performance impact to the other parts working in conjunction with it.

Techniques for Maximizing Software Component Reliability

In the following sections, we cover techniques for maximizing the reliability of your system's software components.

Avoid using "Version 1" and "Beta" software

When purchasing off-the-shelf software products, bypass those that have been just recently written. So-called "Version 1" software is bound to contain many bugs, and you're better off avoiding these applications for business-critical work. Given the pace at which software vendors must release new products to remain competitive, it's understandable that less attention is given to quality, bug-free software than ever before. What's more, configurations are so diverse nowadays that it is extremely difficult to thoroughly test software prior to its public release.

As a way to test software with actual users, many developers release beta versions of their software. These beta versions have most or all of the functionality of the final product, but suppliers freely admit that the applications do not yet work perfectly. Beta software users are supposed to help improve the final product by offering feedback about how the beta software works (or *fails* to work). Beta testing software is not for everyone. Never use it as a means to get free software. Not only is it possible the software will fail to work properly, it might also damage your computer system — and you're on your own if it does.

Don't use shareware or freeware

Nothing is free in the world, not even so called shareware or freeware. These programs, especially if written by unknown authors, may have serious flaws.

- **They may contain virus code** — Virus authors can use shareware or freeware as a carrier. Even if they do not, you still risk virus infection, since shareware and freeware is typically passed freely amongst users, especially if it has been downloaded from the Internet.
- **They may be poorly designed** — The author has nothing to lose (except his reputation) if he writes bad software, since nobody is paying him for it.
- **They may be usable only for a certain amount of time** — Imagine that you've downloaded an especially useful piece of shareware, and you start using it to the point that you become dependent on it. Three months later, the software displays a message that it has expired and you must register in order to continue using it. To register means you must pay for a license, so you still end up paying for it. It might have been better to get the same type of software for a fee, but from a reliable vendor, with better functionality and support.
- **The programs may not scale properly** — Most shareware is designed for low-scale use and deployment. If you begin to use it throughout an enterprise, it may not function as well as you expect.

Buy industry-standard software from reliable vendors

Obviously, reliable software doesn't just happen — it is developed painstakingly by companies that invest extensive time and resources on it. For this reason, you are safer buying software from companies with a record for quality.

Make sure that the software you buy is designed to comply with the standards your system uses. If possible, buy products that have been certified to work within the standard.

Prior to installation, test for viruses

You can never be too cautious when it comes to computer viruses. There have been cases when major software vendors have unknowingly shipped virus infected software. Check for viruses when you introduce something new — and make sure to use *up-to-date* antivirus software.

Provide menus and other ways to control user inputs

A common source of software errors is user input. If users must provide input, wherever possible, limit their choices by using drop-down selection lists instead of keyboard entry fields. Use mouse-driven menus instead of command-line input. Not only does this approach make your application more user-friendly, it also eliminates the risk of inputs that are incorrect, reduce data quality, or trigger software bugs.

Reuse bug-free components or modules

Encourage programmers to reuse proven software modules, components, parts, and libraries. This saves time *and* improves reliability. Code reuse is growing easier to accomplish, through the use of contemporary object-oriented programming languages such as Java and C++.

Test programs thoroughly

Never implement new software without thorough testing, and always know how to restore your system to its working state if something goes wrong during testing. As you test, pay attention to how the new application affects system performance, ensuring that it does not introduce new problems or bottlenecks. Adequate testing means running the new application at different times of the day, when the system is at different utilization levels.

Run "beta tests" with a controlled set of users

Test new software on a small group of users first, before requiring everyone to use it. Determine whether any problems arise due to the way users work with (or misuse) the application. Beta testing should run for an adequate amount of time to cover most possible user activities.

Install the latest application software fixes judiciously

The manufacturers of off-the-shelf software products often release a multitude of bug fixes, addressing a wide range of issues — serious problems, intermittent problems, problems experienced only under rare circumstances, performance enhancements, even cosmetic improvements and minor new features. In most cases, these fixes are readily available via the Internet. Don't be tempted to install every new fix as it comes out. Only install those that apply to *your* environment. Read the installation notes carefully — some of these fixes may cause unwanted side effects that may impact you more than the original problem ever did.

Install the latest device drivers when available

Operating system and hardware vendors will occasionally make updated device drivers available. In general, we recommend that you install these updates — they often can make significant improvements in both stability and performance.

Upgrade to newer operating systems with caution

When a new operating system version comes out, it often creates excitement, and IT people become over-eager to implement it. Never forget the crucial role operating systems play in maintaining availability. *If it ain't broken, don't change it.*

When you do change, make sure there are compelling business reasons to do so, and that your systems will be compatible with the new version — and powerful enough to support it. It took several years for Windows 95 to become dominant on the business desktop — not because it wasn't superior, but because the installed base of PCs did not have sufficient computing power.

Minimize the use of system utilities

Non-essential system utilities waste system resources, decreasing system performance, and can sometimes cause system instability. In some cases, utilities are necessary — for example, antivirus software. But avoid animated screen savers, sound effects, and other frills, and discourage your users from installing them.

Personnel-Related Techniques for Maximizing Reliability

In the following sections, we cover techniques for maximizing the reliability of the "peopleware" elements of your system.

Ensure high-quality user training

It seems obvious, but it's often taken for granted — make sure users have sufficient knowledge to use your system properly. Many calls to help desks are usage-related, and many problem calls result from improper use of the system. The impact of these problems can range from minor nuisances to major system outages. You can achieve quality training by establishing a skills roadmap and checklist for every major system component, and ensuring that users have acquired the skills on the roadmap *before* they get their hands on the system.

Ensure quality training of support staff members

Naturally, your IT support staffers should be adequately trained to support users and to handle system problems. Since support personnel require deeper skills, you cannot expect all of them to be experts in everything. You can, however, have at least one expert (preferably two, for redundancy) in every major system component. If this is impossible, identify a service provider who can lend expertise for a fee. Consider purchasing maintenance and support contracts not only for hardware, but for software as well.

Be wary of contractual hires

There is a growing industry trend to rely on part-time, casual, or temporary IT staffers. Though the short-term financial benefit of contracting out is obvious, the risks of trouble may be even higher. Contractors have less experience with your information systems, and may need to spend a great deal of time "experimenting" on the job. Even more importantly, since they know they won't be working for you long, they may be less motivated to do quality work.

Environment-Related Techniques for Maximizing Reliability

In the following sections, we cover techniques for maximizing the reliability of the environment in which your system must operate.

Install Automatic Voltage Regulators (AVRs)

Electronic equipment rarely fails. If it does, it's likely an external factor caused the failure — most often, the quality of electricity. Installing an automatic voltage regulator (AVR) device between your computer equipment and power source can dramatically reduce the likelihood of equipment failures. AVRs attenuate the electrical spikes that can occur when nearby electric devices are switched on or off, when thunderstorms are present, or when faulty conditions exist in the electric power plant or the grid delivering power to your location. These spikes, if left unhampered, can damage your equipment and eventually cause it to fail. Danger signs of power-related problems include equipment that often fails at the same time of the day or week; multiple failures at the same location; or intermittent problems that are otherwise difficult to track down.

Use adequate air-conditioning equipment

When choosing the type of cooling equipment for your computer systems, use the right type for the right reasons. When you need to cool a room 24 hours a day, 7 days a week, use the large package-type air conditioners, not small window units that aren't designed to operate continuously, and are easy to overstress. You need a reliable source of cool air that will continue to work regardless of the temperature outside.

Some Reliability Indicators for Suppliers

In the following sections, we offer strategies for choosing quality suppliers.

Time in business

When a company has been doing the same thing for a long time (and continues to make money at it), it's likely they have quality products.

Quality certification

ISO 9000/9001 certification is a rating given by an ISO-accredited third party that has thoroughly audited a company's business processes, and assures the outside world that these processes meet high standards and are followed (at least at the time of the audit). Quality-assured processes are likely (but *not* certain) to produce quality products. What is important is that companies which go through the trouble of ISO certification most likely have a culture of quality, and that *does* lead to reliable products.

Industry awards

Look to third-party organizations for independent analyses or reviews of a supplier's products and services. Companies with *one* award-winning product show promise, but companies that have garnered multiple awards over a long period of time offer even stronger assurance of high quality.

Don't just count the awards received — evaluate the awarding organization. Is it credible? Unbiased? Look to nonprofit and professional organizations more than commercial entities such as trade publications and Web sites, especially if the commercial organizations are supported by the firms receiving the awards (e.g., through advertising, joint marketing, co-selling). A quality awards body will always explain its criteria for winner selection.

Consider the scope and breadth of nominees the award winner was chosen from. We've often seen quality products lose to inferior ones simply because the quality products were not included in the evaluation. This might have occurred for several reasons. The awards body might not have sufficient funds to purchase all products for evaluation.

Or perhaps not all vendors were contacted, or vendors were given insufficient time to submit products. In some cases, the best products were simply introduced too late to be evaluated.

Peer recommendation

Ask those whom you trust or work closely with. They may have first-hand experience with the suppliers you intend to deal with, including direct experience with vendor staff members in sales and support.

Warranty and support

We always like getting products with quality *guaranteed*, not just promised. The optimal warranty includes time *and* materials, and lasts longer than competitors' warranties. If a supplier is not willing to back its product with a quality warranty, why should *you* shoulder the risk of purchasing it?

▶ Programming to Minimize Failures

What is good application design? In today's fast-paced, user-focused IT environment, many people will answer simply: *good application design does what the user asked for, and it works.* Yes, these are elements of good design, but they're far from the whole story. The applications works now, but are you confident it will continue to work tomorrow, or the next day?

Good application design should plan for future growth, and, more importantly, consider potential problems and prevent them from occurring. To accomplish this, developers must make a conscious effort to achieve four key attributes: correctness, robustness, extensibility, and reusability.

Correctness

Correctness means that an application performs according to specifications, doing what it was intended to do. To ensure correctness, follow these steps.

Ensure user requirements are adequately determined

To find out what the user really needs, the secret is (drum roll please) to ask them! Sometimes, IT staffers become so enamored of their skills, they make assumptions about their users' preferences. This leads to incorrect specifications, since IT professionals tend to favor technical rather than user-oriented features.

Much rework, redesign, and conflict between users and application developers can be avoided by simply investing sufficient time up front in listening to users and their managers. They will tell you what tasks they need to perform, what goals they need to achieve, which features are most important to them — and which features would be confusing or useless.

For instance, a manager might ask for a feature that computes a monthly loan amortization. A user might tell you the most convenient way to input the data that will be used in the calculation (e.g., choose dates by clicking on a calendar). The user might also tell you what corresponding information should be displayed alongside (e.g., borrower's credit history). The manager can tell you which types of data should be disallowed (e.g., minimum and maximum loanable amounts).

If you fail to speak with either the user or the manager, you'll end up with an application that fails to do everything the business requires, or is never used because users find it too cumbersome.

Prototype the application prior to detailed coding

Before you create all the program code for the application, perform hands-on usability testing with a prototype that simulates how the application will actually run — in essence, "painting a picture" of the final application. With prototyping, you can get a better understanding of the factors that will encourage the user to work with the system, design points that are (or aren't) acceptable, and other key details. Your objective here is to make sure that the way you *think* the application should be operated is in fact what the user really wants.

Revalidate user requirements midway through the project

Pause partway through a complex application design project to ensure that the future final product is still of value to the user. This is especially important in lengthy projects, projects that involve rapidly-changing technology, or projects that have been subject to extensive user-driven changes.

Beta test prior to wide-scale deployment

Safeguard against widespread system and user problems by testing a beta version of the application in a controlled environment with a small set of users. By doing so, you can discover problems that weren't noticed during development. Choose beta testers who represent a good mix of your entire user community, with varying roles and experience levels.

Robustness

Robustness means an application can continue to function outside its specifications. A robust application can better tolerate unexpected conditions, avoiding failures or outages. Robustness is achieved by the following means:

Test against out-of-bounds values

Don't assume that your software will never encounter unusual operating conditions such as invalid data inputs and user entry errors. Test against these and other potential errors: long data input, null data entry, zero values, and high numbers. Design your application to respond to these errors, either by ignoring them, filtering them, or generating error alerts to users. No out-of-bounds value should cause an application to run differently or erroneously.

Trap errors and prevent them from propagating

Anticipate and "contain" error conditions so they do not impact your running programs. You can code your applications so they bypass the problem; or report it to the user and wait for him to fix the problem; or automatically terminate, first closing all open files properly.

For example, if a corrupted data file is encountered, the application should inform the user of the existence of the bad data and ask for what to do next (e.g., "data error reading drive A: Abort, Retry,

Ignore?") Another example is the way Windows "kills" a running application if it executes an invalid instruction (e.g., "A fatal error has occurred. Program will be terminated.").

Anticipate external changes

A good application should be ready to handle external changes outside its control. Examples include changes in date formats, currencies, and units of measures.

Ever wonder why the United States is still avoiding the metric system? Arguably, it's due to the extensive effort required to convert all computer applications to handle a different measurement system — simply because the programmers did not take this shift into consideration.

Similarly, the shift to the Euro currency is giving many programmers sleepless nights, because they did not design their systems to handle such changes smoothly.

Extensibility

Extensibility means an application may easily be adapted to changes in specifications. In today's business environment, user requirements change constantly, making extensibility an absolute necessity. Change is inevitable for these and other reasons:

User changes

Your users may change their requirements. They may hear about an application similar to yours, but with features yours doesn't have. Your users themselves may change, due to a corporate acquisition, buy-out, or merger. The use of temporary workers and contractors also changes your user population.

System platform changes

The operating system or environment on which your application runs could also change. Typically, a new version or type of operating system also offers a new or revamped user interface (e.g., DOS to Windows 3x, Windows 3x to Windows 95/98/NT, even to a lesser degree, Windows 98 to Windows 2000).

Regulatory changes

Your company may also find itself having to adapt to changes in the regulatory environment, including new accounting practices, new currencies, or new tax rules. Changes might be required due to the implementation of quality programs such as Malcolm Baldridge or ISO. New processes and systems might also be required if laws about the archiving of electronic records change.

Budgetary changes

Your resources to support an application or system may suddenly be reduced or eliminated, forcing you to redesign your applications and processes. This type of change could be brought about by external factors, such as abrupt currency devaluations which reduce the buying power of money already set aside for your department's use.

Business volume changes

If business suddenly booms, your application might suddenly have to handle twice as many transactions, deal with an expanded product line, or keep track of more customers and suppliers.

Business demand changes

Your business environment may change dramatically. What if your country's currency suddenly devalued by 1000 times? Will your applications be able to handle values that have spiraled from 1,000,000 to 1,000,000,000?

How is extensibility achieved? Here are just a few examples.

Generous database field sizes

Create database fields that are larger than your current needs, or at least consider the possibility of having to use large data. For example, when creating a currency field, consider planning maximum values in the trillions, not the millions. If your application is suddenly used for the Japanese yen or some other high-number currency, you won't encounter field size problems. At the rate that storage costs are declining, the few extra bytes you use up aren't likely to matter much in the near future anyway. Our rule of thumb: make the maximum size or value at least 50 percent more than your current maximum or largest data.

Design with overcapacity

Design your systems and applications with enough room for growth. This would mean putting extra capacity into the system at the start. If your company has 100 employees, design your system to work fast enough with 200. If you foresee data storage requirements in the gigabytes, design your system to handle terabytes. Extra capacity or capability you design in now won't go to waste — you'll be placing less stress on your system due to the overcapacity.

Place constant values in a look-up table

Never hard-code constant values into your program codes. If you do, and you must change those values in the future, you'll have to plow through every line of code to find all the instances of the value. Instead, define a table of constants your program can refer to as needed. Now, if you need to change a constant, you must do it only once, in the table.

Obvious examples include currency exchange rates and interest rates. Less obvious examples include the number of workdays in a week, and the number of working hours in a day. Right now, the business is standardized on a five-day week, but flextime might be implemented, and some people might find themselves working four ten-hour days.

Reusability

Reusability means that an application, or portions of it, may be used by another application with little or no modification. Reusability is especially beneficial if you have good, stable programs or modules already written. Reusability makes it faster and easier to design new applications, and allows you to improve the reliability of these applications from the outset. Reusability has long been a dream of program developers, and the use of object-oriented programming languages may be the solution.

In object-oriented programming, both code and data references are stored together in an **object**. Instead of executing program instructions linearly, one after another, in object-oriented programming you call on objects to give you the data or result that you need, paying no attention to what goes on inside the object. This approach is called **encapsulation**. All communications to and from objects is done by **messages**. The code that is executed when a message is sent is called its **method**.

Code reusability comes into play when objects are arranged into **classes**, and all new objects that are part of that class can inherit the characteristics of that class. This property that gives all members of a subclass the same behavior as its parent class is called **inheritance**.

Some better-known object-oriented programming languages are:

- **C++** — An object-oriented version of the C language. Existing programs written in C can be incorporated, with some modifications, simplifying the conversion from C to C++.
- **Java** — This is a relatively new programming language gaining popularity in businesses, in part because it can run inside most Internet browsers. Java uses similar syntax to C++ but eliminates memory pointers. It runs on any brand of computer that supports a Java Virtual Machine, and JVMs are built into most current web browser software, including Netscape Communicator and Internet Explorer.
- **Smalltalk** — Another popular object-oriented programming language. It was designed as an object-oriented programming environment from the ground up. Examples of Smalltalk products are VisualAge, VisualWorks, and Visual Smalltalk. This language is easier to use than C++, but programs written with it run slower.

▶ Implement Environmental Independence Measures

Implement techniques for eliminating outages caused by external factors outside of your control, such as electric power, temperature, humidity, and other environmental factors.

Use Power Generators

In most countries, the likelihood of power outages is remote, especially in highly industrialized cities. But they still happen once in a while, and having a standby generator will save you from hours of system outages.

In 1997, a major power outage in San Francisco lasted eight hours. Many computer systems were unprepared, and remained shut down until power was restored. Many businesses were affected. Even the global Internet was not spared from problems, as many major gateways serving international Internet Service Providers are located in the San Francisco area. Eventually, power was restored and the cause of the outage was determined — a technician mistakenly cut a major power line, causing several power plants to shut down, one after another.

Use Independent Air-Conditioning Units

To protect your equipment from high heat and humidity, install air-conditioning units designed to operate for as long as your systems are running. These can also control the humidity level of your computer room — essential for maintaining the integrity of stored magnetic tapes.

It is best to have an air-conditioning unit that is independent of the building cooling system. One reason is that the chance of a failure is higher for the building's equipment since it is much more complicated equipment. Secondly, if you must operate your system 24 hours a day, 7 days a week, it will generally be less costly to run your own cooling systems than to use your building's cooling equipment.

Use Fire Protection Systems

Fire protection systems should be installed to minimize the damage in case fire breaks out in your computer facility. Install a protection system independent of your building's system, because you don't want your equipment damaged by accident if the system is triggered by a fire elsewhere in the building. At most, have an alarm indicator linked to the facilities' system, so your people are made aware of the emergency situation.

Use Raised Flooring

Raised flooring is the norm for mainframe computer systems because of the amount of copper wiring that must pass between equipment. With the arrival of smaller midrange and server computers, the need for raised flooring was lessened. However, we still advocate its use for these reasons:

- Raised flooring moves cables away from human traffic, eliminating problems caused by people tripping over cables.
- Raised flooring simplifies cable management. Since you are not space constrained, you can organize your cables more efficiently. Periodic checks, relabelling, and inventory-taking is simplified, as well.
- You can pass cool air inside the raised flooring, distributing cooling more evenly throughout the computer room.
- Your equipment is better protected from flooding since it is higher than the base flooring.

Install Equipment Wheel Locks

Mainframe equipment commonly uses lockable caster wheels that prevent the equipment from moving around by accident or by force of nature, as in an earthquake. If you can install caster wheels beneath your equipment or racks, by all means do so.

Locate Computer Room on the Second Floor

You will have more peace of mind if you know that your computer facility is unlikely to flood. Therefore, locate your computer room on the second or third floor — not on the ground floor or, even worse, in the basement.

▶ Utilize Fault Avoidance Measures

Among the most sophisticated reliability techniques are those that seek to predict failures and take preventive measures before the failures occur. Some examples of fault avoidance are discussed in the following sections.

Analyzing Problem Trends and Statistics

One powerful contribution of an effective Problem Management discipline is a repository of past problems that you can use to project future problems. This "data mining" activity should be done regularly and diligently. Only with experience can you gain the skills you need to accurately predict problems.

For example, you may analyze reports and discover that one department is reporting many usage-related problems. What can you predict? You can foresee that people in that department will start to make mistakes, such as accidentally deleting or overwriting critical files, improperly shutting down applications, and inputting incorrect data, thereby impacting overall system availability. You can respond by conducting user training. After you do, you're likely to see a significant decrease in help desk calls, while at the same time reducing the risk of usage-related outages.

Or, you might see a particular hardware component encountering many problems lately. What do you do? You can schedule it for preventive maintenance, buy a spare of the same equipment and have it readily available, or retire the equipment completely. Whatever solution you choose, you've taken proactive steps to prevent a systemwide outage from occurring.

Use of Advanced Hardware Technologies

Some equipment now contains built-in temporary error analysis and predictive failure algorithms. An example: hard disk drives that use the SMART standard (Self-Monitoring, Analysis, and Reporting Technology). SMART monitors a drive to detect when predetermined error thresholds are exceeded. If it detects this, it sends error codes to the hard disk adapter, which forwards alerts to management software that alerts the administrator. The administrator can then replace the drive during scheduled downtime.

Use of Software Maintenance Tools

Several software utilities, especially data storage utilities, can perform reliability tests and offer recommendations based on the frequency of errors found. There are also tape analyzers that read data tapes and check their ability to retain data. You can specify a "safety" level beneath which you'll be notified that a tape or component should be fixed or replaced.

Network management software can provide statistics on communication and line errors, to help you identify communication links or resources that are about to fail. Our experience is that communications equipment rarely fails suddenly — if you look at error logs preceding the failure, you'll usually find many temporary or recovered errors.

▶ Summary

This chapter discussed several techniques for increasing system reliability:

- Using reliable components
- Programming to minimize failures
- Implementing environmental independence measures
- Using fault avoidance measures

There is nothing especially technical about these techniques. Most are common sense. Too often, we seek complicated, elegant solutions to simple problems. Sometimes we like to show off our skills by doing things we know others won't understand, so we appear more capable and sophisticated than we really are.

We hope that the discussion in this chapter has proven to you the value of good old common sense and practicality. Remember that in the end, you will get the credit if your system is useful, responsive, and stable.

Special Techniques for System Recoverability

▶ Automatic Fault Recognition

In this chapter, we will discuss several techniques for designing more recoverable systems. The first is to detect the presence of a faulty condition as quickly as possible — ideally, before it impacts the entire computing system. If you can localize the fault to a small portion of your system, you have a better chance to recover from it sooner. There are many ways to detect and localize faults. Many are dependent on the specific technologies and platforms you have in place. We will discuss a few examples as illustrations.

Parity Checking Memory

Most computer systems use some form of memory or storage parity checking to detect data integrity problems. With parity memory checking, if a single bit of storage is in error, a parity error is generated. A single-bit error may be temporary, but it could be a sign of a degrading system component.

Memory may encounter two possible types of errors: "soft" errors due to radiation-induced bit switching; and "hard" errors due to the unexpected deterioration of a memory chip. Soft errors do not indicate lasting damage to the memory board, but they do corrupt programs or data if they are not immediately corrected. Hard errors demand physical repairs.

When a parity problem occurs, the operating system usually terminates the running application to prevent further damage to the system. Parity-check conditions should be investigated as soon as possible.

We have seen many users of personal computers turn parity checking feature off, or purchase computer memory without parity checking to save money. They stand to waste more money if they encounter a serious problem that could have been anticipated had they used parity checking.

ECC Memory

Parity checking is limited to detecting single storage bit errors. It cannot identify which bit in a byte of data is in error, or correct the problem. To overcome these limitations, a newer type of memory was introduced for critical computer systems — Error Checking and Correcting (ECC) memory. ECC can detect and correct an error before it impacts your system. More expensive than conventional memory, ECC is primarily found in high-end workstations or servers.

Data Validation Routines

User entries should always be validated to ensure that bad input is immediately spotted, and not stored or acted upon. Many types of data validation can be performed, including:

- **Checking if data is valid, based on a table of possible inputs —** For example, you can check the department location input of a user by comparing it with a list of your company's departments. If no match is found, generate an error message like: "You entered an invalid department name. Please correct your entry."

- **Checking for valid data type** — For example, if you are expecting a numeric input, any non-numeric entry should be immediately rejected.
- **Checking for valid data format** — This check is especially useful for date entries. Ensure that your desired input format is the same as what the user enters. For example, if you want dates entered in the months/day/year format (e.g., 3/27/01), you can check the month field and reject entries greater than 12.
- **Checking for valid data range** — If you expect positive numbers, reject negative inputs immediately.
- **Checking for valid data sizes** — Limit the amount of data that may be inputted by the user. We've heard of cases when an application unintentionally accepted a long PIN code entry in an Automated Cash Teller Machine, and the software became confused, allowing user to withdraw too much money. A common hacker practice is to attempt large data inputs, in the hope a program will malfunction, providing unauthorized access to sensitive resources.

▶ Fast Recovery Techniques

Additional techniques are available to speed recovery from failures that have been discovered automatically. For example:

- **Journaled File System** — High-availability operating systems, such as IBM's AIX for the RS/6000 line of computers, track all file system changes in a Journaled File System (JFS) log. If an error is detected during a system restart, the JFS log can be analyzed immediately, and the file system can be repaired by rolling back the changes. This repair can occur much more quickly than in a system without an automated correction system.
- **Automatic restart capability** — Windows NT and Windows 2000 can automatically restart if a system crash occurs. If the system crashes during unattended hours (e.g., late at night), it can restore itself to operating condition without the intervention of a system operator. Users accessing the server are spared from having to experience a prolonged outage.

- **Recovered file technique** — Some applications can recover what a user was doing shortly before his application or system was abnormally terminated, drastically reducing the amount of work that must be redone.

▶ Minimizing Use of Volatile Storage Media

A little-known technique to aid in recovering from an outage is to minimize the use of storage media that is susceptible to loss of data, by committing new or modified data permanent storage as soon as possible. By volatile storage, we refer to those devices that lose the data stored in them when power to the system is lost. Some possible ways to do this are:

Regular Database Updates to Central Storage

When you work on a database system, especially in an enterprise environment, your changes may not be immediately posted on the central database repository. This is especially true for users connected via a wide area network whose bandwidth limits the degree of concurrency between data seen by users and that stored in the central server. Design systems like these to update the central server with new data as often as possible. Then, if the network connection to the user is lost, or the user computer goes down, less data must be reinputted.

Automatic File-Save Features

If possible, configure your desktop applications to automatically save changes to the hard disk regularly (e.g., 10 minutes). This feature is fairly common in today's off-the-shelf software packages. Turn the feature on by default, or remind users to leave the feature enabled. The advantage is obvious — if a computer suddenly crashes, the user must only redo any work done since the last automatic save.

▶ Summary

This chapter introduced several techniques for improving system recoverability by automating the detection or response to problems. The techniques cited include:

- Automatic fault recognition
- Fast recovery techniques
- Minimizing the use of volatile storage

These techniques are more technical than those in the previous chapter, requiring a deeper understanding of your system resources and software. Review your most common types of problems systematically, seeking to identify recoverability solutions. Remember that the best way to increase recoverability is to minimize the damage in the first place, by detecting the problem as early as possible and preventing its spread to other system components.

Special Techniques for System Serviceability

▶ ## Online System Redefinition

The first technique for improving system serviceability is to deploy equipment that can be serviced without bringing down the entire computing system. Online system maintenance gives you the flexibility to perform repair work at a convenient time, instead of waiting until there are no users at all on the system (an increasingly rare occurrence) or deliberately causing an outage.

Add or Remove I/O Devices

Many newer computer systems allow you to install or remove input or output devices without powering down the computer.

For example, Sun Microsystems' Solaris operating environment has a Dynamic Reconfiguration (DR) feature that enables you to dynamically attach and detach system boards in a live system without halting the operating system or any user program. With Solaris 7, the addition or removal of CPUs and memory boards is also supported.

189

In PCs, the Universal Serial Bus (USB) provides on-the-fly "Plug-and-Play" support for external computer peripherals. With USB, there is no need to install hardware electronic "cards" inside the computer — a task that requires the system to be powered down. Instead, you connect a USB device to the USB port of your computer, and (assuming your operating system supports USB, as Windows 98 and Windows 2000 do), the system immediately recognizes the new device.

Up to 127 devices can run simultaneously on one USB port. Many types of USB devices are now on the market, including modems, keyboards, mice, CD-ROMs, printers, and even telephones.

Selectively Power Down Subsystems

In IBM mainframes and peripherals, you can power down the portion of the computer system you need to repair, by placing it in Service Mode condition. For example, you can choose to power down an I/O channel to connect or remove an I/O device. You can also place a single storage device in a complex storage subsystem into Service Mode, allowing you to replace, reformat, or diagnose it as needed.

Commit or Reject Changes

With IBM's AIX operating system, you can apply and test changes, then commit or reject them later, based on the test's results. This feature is especially useful if you do not have a spare test system for your changes. The operating system maintains a copy of all the system files, new and old. If your change causes problems, you can use the AIX reject process to undo the changes and restore the operating system to its previous working state. If the change is successful, you can permanently delete the obsolete system files.

▶ Informative Error Messages

One easy yet overlooked technique for improving serviceability is to provide complete and accurate information to users, administrators, and service personnel. If you are creating custom software or designing management tools, provide comprehensible, detailed messages about the current system condition — messages that can easily be used to track and fix problems. The next sections present some guidelines.

Use Standard Corporate Terminology

Throughout your organization, including IT staff and users, establish a common set of terminology. If possible, publish a corporate IT glossary. For example, to describe the mainframe computer in your main computer room, do you use *host*, *server*, or *mainframe*? What is the difference between a *failure* and an *outage* — which one lasts longer? When you use a common language in discussing problems, you eliminate confusion and misinterpretation.

Adopt Terms Already Used by Common Applications

Wherever possible, follow the terminology used by common software programs, as your users will already be familiar with this terminology. For example, to load a file, use the word *open*, as used in most Microsoft Office programs, instead of using *load*, *get*, *read*, or *process*. To describe copying data into memory, use *paste*, not *drop* or *put*. Your users will have an easier time learning your terminology, and won't have to unlearn what they already know.

Tell What, Why, Impact, and How

The error messages you create should accomplish four goals. First, they should tell the user what went wrong. Second, to the extent possible, they should explain why the error occurred. Third, they should inform the user of the impact of the error. Finally, they should help the user recover by advising what to do next.

Let's use a classic user error as an example — saving to an empty diskette drive. The classic error message reads: "drive not ready. Abort, retry, ignore?" or "error reading drive A. Abort, retry, ignore?" It's easy to improve on this. A better message might read: "Error trying to save to diskette because no diskette was found or disk drive not functioning. Changes to your data were not successfully saved. Do you want to Abort ("I'll save my data later"), Retry ("I inserted a diskette or have checked the disk drive and want to try again"), or Ignore ("I have no other recourse but to try to continue saving even if I lose some of my data").

Another example: "You have entered an invalid date. Please ensure that the date is of the form MM/DD/YYYY. Also check that the date exists (e.g., there is no 02/31/YYYY). If the problem still persists, please report error code 345, including all actions done, to the help desk at local 343."

Implement Context-Sensitive Help

Your help information should be context-sensitive — linked to what the user was doing when he asked for help. The last thing the user wants to do is search through help files to find what he is looking for.

Microsoft Office applications, for example, have a help facility that turns your cursor into a question mark. When you click on a screen element, a pop-up text message explains the purpose of the screen element you clicked on. Microsoft Office can also display an animated assistant who runs in the background, trying to anticipate what you need to do, and providing task-sensitive help. For example, if you are idle for some time, the assistant appears to offer help.

Give Options for Viewing More Detailed Error Information

If you're worried that context-sensitive help will clutter your application, at least provide a short problem description, with a button to click for more detailed information. This gives users the option of getting more information if they want it. In the first example above, your error message might state: "Error while trying to save data. Abort, Retry, Ignore, or Details (recommended)." In the second example, it might state: "Error processing data — bad date. Press 'Y' to see more information, then consult the help desk if you still have problems."

Make Error Information Available
After the Error Has Been Cleared

Service personnel are often frustrated to discover that error messages have been cleared by users before the service staff can read and act upon them. Store all error messages in an error log file. The technician can simply view the contents of the log file to find all the information they need to begin troubleshooting the problem. When you generate error logs, you should:

- **Include as much detail as possible,** including at least *what* happened, and *why* it happened.
- **Include additional information** such as the module that was running when the error occurred, and how the user responded.
- **Timestamp the error record** with the exact date and time of the error.

▶ Complete Documentation

Information about system resources should be available to the service provider to facilitate the repair process and shorten the outage. This may be common sense, but we repeatedly see service staffers have to mount major investigations simply to discover the configuration details of the systems they're working on. In the following sections, we define what we mean by "complete documentation."

Have a Manual of Operations On Hand

Maintain a complete instructional guide for performing your system's key maintenance and operational tasks. This manual can serve as a learning tool for new staff members, a reminder for existing staff, and a guide for those unfamiliar with your system who may be called upon to assist in service or support. You might even have a version of the manual for users, excluding information about sensitive resources and procedures. Your manual should at least cover:

- How to bring up and shutdown the system
- How to take resources off line then back on line
- How to manage job queues
- How to back up and restore data
- How to run diagnostic tools
- System configuration data

Your manual should cover every operating system and environment used in your system.

Write Basic Problem Isolation and Recovery Guides

Provide staff members with guidance on detecting and correcting common problems they may encounter. Discuss what could go wrong, how to bypass the problem, and how to fix it. Build your knowledge base over time, drawing upon your repository of past problems recorded and solved by the help desk.

Provide System Configuration Diagrams

A crucial piece of system documentation is an accurate, up-to-date diagram of how your system resources are interconnected. With it, service personnel can immediately narrow down the source of a problem, identify other components that may have been affected, and plan for making repairs without impacting other system resources unnecessarily.

A basic system configuration diagram shows all your hosts and servers, the devices connected to them, and the networking equipment that ties them together. It identifies which sets of users are connected to which devices, where those devices are located, and how the devices are addressed. It also details connections between devices, showing ports or connectors, network addresses, and corresponding cable labels. Consistent with these diagrams, you should maintain a cable inventory list containing cable names, where they connect from, and where they connect to (see discussion below).

Label Resources

Label all your system resources. In conjunction with the configuration diagram, the labels tell you that the physical resource is what it claims to be — especially if you own many identical components in the same location. Normally, label your resource with the same unique name that you use to refer to it in system definition files and applications.

Typically, the equipment type is used as part of the name, joined with a number or letter that represents either the quantity or address of that equipment. For example, you could have printer devices named *Printer01* or *PrinterA*. You can also attach the function of the device or its location, such as *MITServer* or *MktgServer*.

Don't forget to label cables as well. Power cables, network cables, phone cables, and other special cables can be hard to identify if there is a "spaghetti" of them all over the place. Place a label on *both* ends of the cable. Assign a name to the cable, such as *UTP01*, *Power001*, or *Tel0001*. Then, combine this name with information about where the cable came from and where it goes, like *UTP01 From: MktgHUB01 Port one To: MktgPC01 LAN card* (i.e., this is a UTP cable named UTP01, connecting from Marketing department LAN hub one going to the LAN card of Marketing department PC number 1).

Provide a Complete Technical Library

Make sure that you have all the manuals of every type of system resource you have, including off-the-shelf software, operating systems, in-house applications, and hardware devices. These manuals should be located together. Maintain hard copies of electronic forms of documentation, in case the computers they reside on become unavailable.

▶ Installation of Latest Fixes and Patches

Many hardware products with built-in firmware encounter problems that were not seen during the development cycle. As a result, manufacturers often release firmware fixes to address these problems. These fixes should be installed prior to performing extensive repair work, if applicable to your particular condition. It is important to install firmware fixes first, because:

- The problem you are experiencing might already have been solved by the patch or fix.
- Manufacturers and service providers can only provide accurate repair information and conduct correct diagnosis if your product is at current level (with all current fixes installed).
- Fixes sometimes address recently-discovered security holes or exposures. They can therefore eliminate problems caused by third-parties seeking to compromise the security of your system (i.e., hackers)

▶ Summary

Specialized techniques for improving serviceability make it easier to repair system resources that are experiencing an outage. In this chapter, we have discussed the following techniques:

- Online system redefinition
- Use of informative error messages
- Complete documentation
- Installation of the latest fixes and patches

With experience, you will be able to identify new techniques to lessen the repair time of problems that recur every now and then. Note that bypassing a problem is not the same as solving it. Many IT staff members implement temporary bypass measures when a problem arises and never bother to install a permanent fix. Eventually, the bypass measure leads to other problems, either because the bypass involves doing something not recommended by the manufacturer, or because the bypass has not been adequately documented.

Special Techniques for System Manageability

▶ Use Manageable Components

Let us digress for a moment. What makes the ideal *employee* easy to manage? First of all, they should be honest with you, capable of telling you how they are, what they can and cannot do, and what problems they are currently facing. Second, your employee should be able to follow your instructions, as well as company rules and guidelines — and do so consistently. Third, your ideal employee can communicate with all levels of the management hierarchy if needed, is comfortable escalating issues and concerns, and provides valuable suggestions. Finally, he handles tasks delegated to him with no management guidance, doing the job on his own, and achieving results consistently.

The same traits that make employees easy to manage also make system components easy to manage. There are four main requirements:

- **The component can provide valuable data regarding itself** — Any resource that must be managed must have accessible information about its configuration, features, and current state. This capability eliminates the need to physically inspect the resource — and possibly take it offline — to determine its capabilities. The component should be able to provide information:

– with respect to *configuration:*
- Amount of memory installed
- Type of processor
- Firmware data, such as version and date of manufacture
- Software version, along with author and programming language used
- Number of ports, address range

– with respect to *features:*
- Communication speed capabilities
- Options installed

– with respect to *current state:*
- Online/offline status
- Error information
- Current users and connections
- Current settings of options

- **The component can implement management policies and activities** — The managed resource must perform management-related tasks as specified by the managing system. Such tasks could include health checks, error logging, activation/reactivation of features and resources, and similar activities.

- **The component can communicate with a management application** — The managed resource must be able to exchange data with the managing system, sometimes via its own proprietary communication protocol, but ideally by implementing an industry standard for systems management protocols, as discussed below.

- **The component can be managed remotely from a different location** — A key requirement for system manageability is the ability of the managed resource to be controlled by an external system. This controlling activity can be done via activation/deactivation of software switches, setting of control registers, or remote power on or off. The managed resource needs some form of program logic or electronic interface to provide these features. Without the aid of humans, purely mechanical devices are not manageable, since there is no cost-effective way for the switches and levers to be activated remotely.

Stated simply, system components must provide two-way feedback mechanisms. Years ago, these took the form of status lights, gauges, and audible signals, and required on-premises inspection. Now, in the digital, Internet era, it is theoretically easy to design products that provide feedback. Until recently, however, it was common for these features to be eliminated to cut costs. Fortunately, common approaches for providing feedback — in the form of systems management standards — are now becoming universal.

The need to manage information systems in an orderly and systematic manner arose from the growing complexity of computers and networks. The first protocol to address these management requirements was SNMP. Basic and crudely designed, it delivered an immediate solution to pressing management problems while other, more complex and powerful network management protocols were being designed.

Building on SNMP's framework, SNMPv2 and the Common Management Information Protocol (CMIP) were introduced in the 1980s. Of the two, CMIP was more complex and feature-rich.

When PCs moved raw computing power onto users' desktops, it quickly became essential to manage them. PCs contain their own intelligence, and are capable of independent operation. SNMPv2 and CMIP could not accommodate their unique requirements, so a new standard, the Desktop Management Interface (DMI), was introduced.

Simple Network Management Protocol (SNMP)

SNMP is a systems management standard that grew in popularity not because it provided all the needed features and functions, but because there was no better alternative for quite some time. SNMPv2 eventually came out, improving on the existing foundation of SNMP.

With SNMP, network management information is communicated by way of messages between managing and the managed resources. Five kinds of messages are used to read data from the network device, change its settings, or signal the managing resource that an event has occurred at the device (the Trap signal). To check on the status of a network device, for example, you send a Read message to the device. A Trap message might be generated when the network device is shut down.

SNMP stores information about connected devices in a Management Information Base (MIB). The MIB contains the following information:

- The name of the field or variable
- The type of data stored in the field or variable (e.g., string, integer)
- The behavior of the field (e.g., read-only or read-write)
- The value of the field or variable

Since only simple messages and information are exchanged, SNMP introduces little additional network traffic — a major reason for its popularity. Today, most network devices support SNMP in one way or another.

One main disadvantage of SNMP is that it is not secure. Hackers can easily intercept or send SNMP messages, causing the unauthorized shutdown of network devices. However, SNMPv2 addresses these security concerns.

SNMPv2 also addresses the second major disadvantage of SNMP — that it is too simple to adequately represent the state of more complex devices. SNMPv2 supports additional types of messages, and allows the manipulation of the fields or variables in the managed devices.

Despite SNMPv2's obvious benefits, it has not yet been adopted as widely as SNMP. Many of today's network devices support SNMP along with SNMPv2's security extensions.

Common Management Information Protocol (CMIP)

CMIP was intended to replace SNMP by providing features and functions not found on either SNMP and SNMPv2. Messages are also passed around to read, set, manipulate, and trap events, and there are now 11 types of messages. In CMIP, the variables are complex data structures with many attributes, like:

- **Variable attributes** — its characteristics, such as data type, read/write capability

- **Variable behaviors** — the actions of the variable that can be triggered
- **Notifications** — the event report that can be sent whenever a specified event occurs

The biggest difference between CMIP and SNMP is that CMIP's variables can not only provide information to and from network devices, but can also perform tasks otherwise impossible to accomplish with SNMP. For example, with CMIP you can specify that a message be sent to an external resource whenever a certain threshold is reached. The external resource need not track whether the threshold is exceeded — the CMIP device handles tracking.

Security is also an area in which CMIP excels. CMIP can perform authorization checks, access controls, and keep security related logs.

Unfortunately, CMIP's strength is one reason for its slow adoption. To fully implement CMIP in a device requires much more effort and cost, in extra intelligence, hardware, software, and specialized programming skills.

Desktop Management Interface (DMI)

The DMI specification, created by the Desktop Management Task Force (DMTF), adds manageability to desktop computers and associated peripherals and software.

DMI collects information from DMI-compliant products and stores the data in a Management Information Format (MIF) database. A Service Layer then makes this information available to systems management applications as requested. These management applications can query, change, control, and track the various components of a desktop personal computer system. The Service Layer acts like a bridge between the managing applications and the managed components.

The information that can be communicated includes:

- BIOS, system board, and processor information
- Cache and standard memory configuration
- Ports, system slots, and on-board devices information
- The contents of system event logs

Common Information Management Format (CIM)

CIM acts as a model for presenting information about system resources that is independent of any particular implementation such as SNMP, CMIP, or DMI. CIM's advocates hope that CIM will allow multiple management applications to share information about their managed resources, making Distributed Systems Management a reality.

Under CIM, management data is collected, stored, and analyzed using a common CIM format that provides room for special product-specific information.

CIM is composed of two parts: the CIM Specification and the CIM Schema. The CIM Specification describes the language, naming conventions, and mapping to the other management models such as SNMP's MIBs and DMI's MIFs. Using an object model, CIM models use classes, properties, and methods to deal with a resource's management information.

The CIM Schema supplies a set of classes within which it is possible to organize the available information about the managed resources. Five base classes are specified: systems, applications, networks, devices, and physical. Extensions are available for unique environments, making the CIM model extensible well into the future.

Wired for Management (WfM)

WfM, an alliance led by Intel Corporation, is intended to make Intel Architecture-based computer systems more manageable remotely across networks. WfM facilitates the following areas of systems management: asset management, universal network boot, off-hours maintenance, system diagnosis and repair, and investment protection.

WfM-compliant systems provide information about their hardware and software components, including how much memory is being used. They deliver the information in CIM and DMI formats, enabling widespread acceptance by systems management applications. Asset management, inventory control, and change control can be greatly aided by the comprehensive data WfM provides.

WfM's Preboot Execution Environment (PXE) makes it possible to configure a system remotely. Using boot agent software loaded in the computer's BIOS, a WfM-compliant system can communicate with a remote server and get boot information over the network, making it possible to install and configure an operating system without sending a technician on-site.

Power-saving features are built in, so a computer can go into low-power sleep mode when no user activity is detected for a given period of time. There is also a remote wakeup feature that can automatically power up the system if a control signal is detected in a network card, modem port, or another input device. These features combine to make it possible for a technician to remotely back up data and install software.

WfM-enabled computers aid problem management by automatically generating trouble tickets or problem reports using a format standardized by the Desktop Management Task Force. Combined with WfM's remote boot and power up capabilities, WfM problem management means a technician can troubleshoot (and often fix) a faulty computer from any location on the network or across the Internet.

Finally, since WfM complies with DMI and CIM specifications, WfM systems should retain their manageability for years to come, prolonging their usefulness in the enterprise.

▶ Management Applications

To have a well-managed company, you need more than ideal employees — you need ideal managers, as well. What makes an ideal manager? First, he should be able to view every employee in relation to the entire organization, understanding who is best suited where, how each employee impacts the entire group, and how to maximize each employee's potential. Secondly, the manager must be able to make decisions independently, reflecting the corporate goals and objectives. Finally, he should be able to analyze team performance and create reports that can help higher management create effective long-term strategies and action plans.

The corollary of having manageable system components is having the capability of managing these resources by using *systems management applications*. Like ideal human managers, ideal systems management applications or frameworks must do the following:

- **Monitor and control as many system components as possible** — A problem arising in an unmanaged component can have a serious impact on the stability of interconnected system resources. The more system components you can manage centrally, the more you can increase system availability.

- **Set systems management policies and enforce them across the system, automatically** — The management application must check on the system's health, perform regular housekeeping, and handle other systems management tasks. It should gather configuration data from every resource and continuously monitor for any changes. It should be able to generate problem reports or raise alarms as soon as it detects a problem — even before users are impacted. The overall objective is to automate as many systems management tasks as possible.

- **Generate summary reports and analyze trends** — For a system management application to maximize its value to IT management, it should excel at data gathering, reporting, and analysis. Management applications should have many different types of reports and analysis to make it easier for the IT organization to generate good long-terms plans for improving system availability.

Systems Management Issues

In a nutshell, systems management applications are specialized software that can communicate and control system components. Some of the more pressing systems management issues being addressed today are discussed below.

Deployment

As more remote systems must be managed, and the distance grows between these systems and the core IT organization, IT needs efficient tools for automating the deployment of new applications and systems to remote users. These tools should provide for deployment planning; reliable, speedy distribution of new software or configuration files; and fine-tuning of applications to optimize them for each desktop throughout the organization.

Operations

To help you run a complex, heterogeneous system dispersed across many locations, your systems management tools must automate as many tasks as possible, and provide assistance with other tasks that cannot be fully automated. It should also help you provide more effective support to end users, no matter where they may be using the system.

Security

The complex interfaces between all your applications, databases, operating systems, and other system components leave many potential sources of security-related problems, including unauthorized access and modification of data, compromised data integrity, and partial or total loss of availability. Don't forget that most of the security problems come from within the company. Systems management software should be cognizant of security issues, and help you respond to them. It certainly should *not* worsen security problems by creating unprotected paths to devices and systems within your network.

Automated Systems Management Capabilities

Some of today's most popular automated systems management capabilities are listed below:

- **Remote console facility** — Enables the IT organization to remotely view, explore, and work on remote workstations and computers as if physically in front of the remote device. This capability is useful in troubleshooting problems encountered by the end user. It obviates the need to expend resources of time and money, especially when the enterprise system is large and spread across different geographies.
- **Software distribution** — Enables installation or modification of software from a central location to remote workstations, in real-time, or on a schedule. This approach is clearly faster and more efficient than a support person installing software on site at each workstation. Imagine the tedium (or frenzy) of modifying a hundred or more workstations within a short timeframe.

- **System and application monitoring** — Provides the management application with a view of configuration information, the operational state, and the error logs of the managed resources.
- **Network management** — Enables viewing of the status of all communication links and networking hardware. Also performs some control function over these network elements when necessary, for example, resetting the link if it goes down.

System Management Applications and Frameworks

Several systems management applications and frameworks (suites of applications with a common interface) are now available. Two of the market leaders are discussed in the following sections.

Unicenter TNG (Computer Associates)

Unicenter TNG gives enterprises a single platform for managing their entire information systems, across multiple platforms. It provides end-to-end management that encompasses virtually every system resource: computer systems, networks, desktop computers, databases, and applications. It also seeks to tie different components together, so when you review a particular element of the information system, you can view its physical and network resources, the applications running on it, and the users that are affected. It also provides a business process view of the system, helping administrators answer such questions as, "Why is the payroll system slow?" This process view is useful for performing business impact analysis about the potential unavailability of a system component.

Unicenter TNG prides itself on an advanced, "real-world" user interface that gives system administrators a three-dimensional representation of the systems they are managing. You start off with an overall view of your entire system, with the capability to focus on any portion of the enterprise and view its component resources in detail. Unicenter TNG is highly customizable — you can specify maps to use, define buildings, and manage network and computer layouts. Unicenter TNG's Unispace feature enables you to visualize abstract objects such as processes, databases, jobs, and users.

Unicenter TNG uses object-oriented programming techniques to store and maintain management information about all system resources. You can deploy management agents throughout your enterprise, including intranet and Internet environments, minimizing the need to constantly report system health data to the central management function. These management agents can be set to implement your desired systems management policies, and send alerts to the central management repository as needed. They can also monitor events and status, perform distributed configuration management, and manage storage across different networks.

Unicenter TNG's Auto Discovery feature allows it to automatically discover your network topology and devices, connected computer systems and their hardware and software configurations, databases and applications running on them, and even the users of those systems.

Tivoli (IBM)

The IBM Tivoli Management Environment (TME) provides IT with a unified view of all system resources by creating a framework on which all the other specialized systems management tools reside and interoperate.

TME solves the problem of integrating multiple systems management tools from diverse vendors. For example, if you have network-monitoring software that detects problems and generates alerts, those alerts should be directly usable by your problem management application, which should automatically create problem tickets and start tracking resolution.

Using the TME framework, systems managers can:

- Set resource availability policies (rules, thresholds, auto-responses, notifications, etc.) from a central site or location
- Deploy these policies to thousands of remote systems
- View the status of an entire enterprise network
- Correlate and handle events from a large number of resources
- Automatically correct problems
- Analyze and diagnose the root causes of a problem

- Create policies for corrective actions or escalations
- Extend system management to include custom monitors or event adapters

When Tivoli was an independent company, it gained a strong following throughout the IT community because of its breadth of coverage of support for many types of personal computer products, high-end servers, and peripherals. In the PC-centric client-server world of the 80s, Tivoli provided a proven solution for managing remote distributed resources effectively.

IBM, realizing the potential of the Tivoli product range, acquired the company and integrated it with its own product line, including IBM's SystemView-based systems management product. This enabled Tivoli TME to also manage traditional mainframe and midrange computer systems. The result is a management application that can handle all types of computing resources, including mainframes, servers, network devices, PC desktops, applications, and databases. In addition, the Tivoli Management Framework presents information about the system being managed in a graphical and easy-to-understand manner.

IBM's SystemView is a systems management framework or blueprint for managing primarily IBM products, such as its mainframe, AS/400, and UNIX product lines. SystemView addresses three critical areas: the end-use dimension, the data dimension, and the application dimension.

The end-use dimension provides a consistent user interface for all systems management tools. All SystemView tools present a common appearance and behavior to the user that complies with IBM's Common User Access (CUA) interface.

The data dimension of SystemView defines information types and a format shared by all SystemView-compliant tools and provides facilities for accessing data consistently. It eliminates the need to reenter the same data in different systems management tools.

The application dimension of SystemView defines tools that address six types of systems management activities: business management, change management, configuration management, operations management, performance management, and problem management.

Educate IS Personnel on Systems Management Disciplines

You cannot expect your information system to function properly if the people running the system are unaware of the principles behind the systems management disciplines. The core principles IT managers should be aware of are discussed below.

Business Value of the Information System

IT professionals should have a strong understanding of the company's business functions, and how each function depends on information technology. Only with this understanding can they make the right decisions and set the right priorities for problem resolution and new application development. This understanding will also give IT staff members the proper perspective on new products and technologies, so they don't implement new technologies without a compelling business rationale.

Value of Systems Management Disciplines

IT staff members should be taught how information systems grow in size and complexity as the business grows, and how this growth in complexity makes effective management crucial. They should be taught the basic principles of each system management discipline, and how the disciplines interact with each other.

Principles of Management

More and more IT organizations are realizing that the business and management skills of IT staff members are as important as their technical skills. IT professionals will have a better appreciation for systems management disciplines if they can relate these to basic principles of people and resource management. Because systems management implementation requires members of your IT organization to work together effectively, they should be trained on working in teams.

Basic Numerical Analysis Skills

To generate business cases, perform trend analysis, and do basic cost and investment analysis, IT staff — especially managers and team leaders — need to understand the fundamentals of accounting, return-on-investments analysis, and statistical analysis. Increasingly, IT organizations are run as profit centers, where services are "sold" to users (who may have alternative sources to choose from). This makes financial understanding even more critical.

▶ Summary

In this chapter, we discussed ways to make your system more manageable. Specifically, we looked at:

- Using manageable system components
- Using management applications
- Educating IT staff members on the disciplines of systems management

Since today's information infrastructure is composed of diverse products from multiple vendors, choose products that conform to popular standards for manageability, such as SNMP, CMIP, or DMI. Choose management systems that are widely utilized with the types of computing systems or platforms you're running on. Stick to the same vendor for hardware, software, and management, and you're far less likely to encounter interoperability problems.

Finally, use systems management procedures that are as generic or commonplace as possible. You can use as a guide the systems management procedures recommended by well-known IT organizations such as the Information Systems Audit and Control Association (*http://www.isaca.org*) or the IT Systems Management Forum (itSMF).

All Together Now

We have discussed many different strategies and techniques for increasing system availability. Let us again emphasize that no matter how much money you spend on technical solutions, they will still be ineffective in preventing most outages unless you also implement systems management disciplines effectively.

▶ The Value of Systems Management Disciplines

Just how critical are systems management disciplines in preventing outages? Consider the systems management discipline of problem management. Strong problem management makes the entire system more reliable, because all problems, large and small, are addressed in one way or another. Weak problem management leaves small problems unresolved, until they become major problems that cause outages. Weak project management means many problems are never fully resolved — simply bypassed by people seeking to avoid the "hassles" of formal problem management processes.

211

Failure to implement effective problem management disciplines can cause problems in many other system management disciplines. For example, a failure to resolve problems with non-critical system components may haunt the organization when those components are called upon to work during an emergency recovery procedure. Uncorrected errors in help files, or damaged help files, can cause headaches for support staffers who encounter problems for which they cannot find accurate information, and delay resolution.

Undocumented problem fixes — which violate the key problem management procedure of recording *all* problem-related information — can dramatically reduce system serviceability. Consider an example familiar to most PC users. Imagine that a support professional tweaks the Windows 95/98 system registry to resolve a recurring intermittent system hang, but fails to document the change. Later, a major problem occurs that entails restoring the registry from an older backup. Because the professional in charge of the restore did not know about the registry tweak, the intermittent system hang problem recurred.

Finally, minor problems left unresolved can interact with one another, increasing system instability and reducing system manageability.

By now, you can probably recount more examples yourself. Trust us when we tell you that we have seen enough real-world examples to arrive at a sacred truth of Information Systems management: *The only effective and sustainable way to increase system availability is to tackle people, process, tools, and information issues together.*

▶ Which One First?

By now, you should be ready to identify your high availability challenges, and attack them. If your organization is like most, you'll find many areas that can stand improvement. Your first challenge will be to set effective priorities. Start by attacking system availability problems with the following characteristics:

- **High incidence of outages** — Systems that often experience outages deserve immediate attention — especially systems whose outages cause other systems to fail as well.

- **Critical business functions affected** — Even if a particular application rarely experiences an outage, it may still need to be addressed immediately, if its unavailability impacts a critical business function. Will an outage result in substantial business losses, impair all work in a sensitive department, or lead to data integrity problems for the entire organization?

- **Customer satisfaction directly impacted** — Anything that can cause problems for your customers should be at or near the top of your list. Customer support applications, invoicing systems, and service provisioning systems are prime candidates.

- **Large number of users affected** — The more users are affected (sometimes tracked by the number of help desk complaints received), the greater the non-quantifiable impact to the operations of the company.

- **High costs to recover from a single outage** — A final consideration in setting priorities is the cost of recovering from an outage in each system. For example, if you have a system or application for which there is no in-house repair expertise, and you would have to fly in a specialist at great expense, you'd want to pay special attention to that application.

▶ Analyze Outages

When analyzing opportunities to improve the availability of an existing information system, start by examining past major outages related to this system. In particular, review:

- **What went wrong** — What triggered the outage? What system component failed or introduced problems? Which IT resources need to be improved, enhanced, or replaced? This should not be difficult to determine if you have good problem records.

- **What was done to recover** — Examine the problem management process, the individual involved in the resolution, and special circumstances that might have lengthened the outage or worsened its impact. Your objective is to improve the process, to educate those involved in the process, and to control dependencies. That way, either the problem won't recur, or its impact can be mitigated.

- **What was the root cause of the outage** — It is critical to analyze the outage and identify not only its proximate cause, but its root cause, which may be entirely different. Remember that well-designed information systems already have failsafe mechanisms to prevent outages. If outages nevertheless occur, was the failsafe mechanism ineffective? Were resources to prevent the outage available? Did the individuals involved perform their role correctly?

- **What can be done to prevent the same outage in the future** — Finally, identify measures to ensure the same outage does not happen again, by addressing the root cause you have previously established.

Recall the example outlined in Chapter 5 — even with a UPS and power generator in place, a system fails during a blackout because a technician failed to check the fuel supply before leaving. You wouldn't stop your analysis with the power company's failure to provide electricity. You would look deeper. Has the technician in charge of checking the fuel supply been out sick? Was there a leak in the fuel tank? You would then identify deeper solutions. These might include backup processes for ensuring that fuel levels and the tank itself are checked when the individual with primary responsibility is unavailable. You might also seek an automated solution, such as a fuel monitoring device.

This example perfectly illustrates the fact that even excellent technical solutions can fail if your processes and people are ineffective.

Identify Single Points of Failure

We have already explained the importance of identifying those crucial system components whose failure will cause the entire system to fail — components with no backup, duplicate, or image that can be substituted automatically. A detailed system hardware and application configuration diagram will help you identify what these are.

Common single points of failures are power supplies, telecommunications and network links, application servers, and even data at the user workstation, if it is not centrally backed up.

Exploit What You Have

It's likely that you already own many components with features that can improve their availability, but these features are either unused or underutilized. There may be no need to purchase more advanced products to enhance availability.

Consider today's business PCs. Their BIOSes are likely to have "boot sector virus protection" that traps all attempts to write to the hard disk master boot record, where many computer viruses hide. Have you enabled this feature? How about "memory parity checking" to halt the system if a parity error occurs, which could be a sign of impending memory failure? Have you set the BIOS System Administrator password to prevent any unauthorized changes to your configuration?

We hope the strategies discussed in this book will change the way you perceive your system resources — the first step in maximizing their potential for improving overall system availability.

An Implementation Strategy

Here are our recommendations for a long-term plan to address and manage system availability.

- Stabilize your current system by eliminating all existing problems. Next, address problems that recur regularly, using the outage analysis technique discussed earlier. Stabilizing your system frees you to embark on more advanced availability improvement projects, and increases your credibility amongst end users, peers, and executive management.

- Implement systems management throughout your IT organization. Good systems management practices make it possible to maintain stable systems, and to prevent new types of outages that might otherwise be caused by introducing new technologies or applications. Start with problem management — next introduce change management. (Many problem management/help desk software applications now contain change management features.) Next, address security management, to protect the integrity of your data from both intentional and accidental damage. Your systems management disciplines need not be perfect before you proceed to the next step. Nobody's systems are perfect, since they are implemented by people who will inevitably make mistakes.

- Choose critical system applications or resources to address, addressing those that will impact overall system availability most (as discussed in the previous section).

- Choose which techniques to implement first, starting with reliability, then recoverability, then serviceability, and lastly manageability. (While you may implement manageability techniques last, be aware that automated manageability is a crucial factor in your up-front planning for new systems.) Wherever possible, implement availability techniques that address several of these availability characteristics at once. Your specific choices will depend on your implementation capabilities: available resources, funding, and skills.

▶ Summary

We have finally reached the end of our book. We hope that by this time, you have gained valuable insights for improving your systems' availability. We recognize that we have not covered every individual product you should consider — this is not possible, given the pace at which technology changes. We do hope, however, to have changed your mindset and attitude, away from thinking primarily about products and technology, and towards a focus on *people, process, and organization*. No matter how technically advanced your information system is, it will suffer outages if its users, processes, and support staff do not work together to maintain and maximize availability.

Every year, the challenges of system availability become greater, and more business critical. If you do nothing, system outages will increasingly become:

- **More costly** as systems get larger and end users have higher expectations and greater dependence on the information system.
- **More likely** as complexity increases (greater number of components, more interdependence).

- **Longer** because they will involve more components that need to be debugged, fixed, and restarted.

With your efforts to implement effective system management disciplines, however, you can leverage advances in technology, quality, and standards to dramatically *reduce* outages. Whether your system is centralized or decentralized, host-centric or client-server, mainframe-based or PC-based, systems management disciplines are equally essential.

Finally, remember that improving system availability begins at the application or system design stage. When you choose the product or technology that will be used in your Information System, choose those that implement techniques for higher availability.

Begin with the end in mind, and you're far more likely to achieve your goals. Begin with higher availability as an objective, and you're one step closer to that elusive goal of 100 percent availability.

Availability Features of Selected Products

In this appendix, we've compiled and condensed information about key availability features in many of today's most widely utilized hardware and software platforms. These listings are not intended to be comprehensive. Rather, they are intended to give you a bird's eye view of the high availability capabilities you may already have paid for — features that are already available for you to exploit.

▶ Availability Features of Selected Operating Systems

In the following sections, we review many of the high availability features associated with today's leading operating systems.

Availability Features of Novell NetWare

http://www.novell.com/products/clusters/

The widely used NetWare 4.x and IntranetWare network operating systems have long provided several features for high availability. These are considered next. More recently, Novell has introduced NetWare 5.x, which can be run as a "pure IP" network, eliminating the need to run multiple protocols; or can be run in connection with NetWare 3.x/4.x networks utilizing IPX/SPX. NetWare 5.x high availability features are covered immediately afterwards.

SFT II (System Fault Tolerance level 2) or mirroring/duplexing

Data on one hard disk can be duplicated on another hard disk on the same I/O channel (for mirroring) or on separate I/O channels (for duplexing). Failure in one drive automatically causes the duplicate disk to take over, preventing an outage from occurring. SFT II allows up to eight drives to be mirrored together.

SFT III (System Fault Tolerance level 3)

SFT III makes full computer server mirroring possible. When a server hardware failure occurs, automatic failover to the functioning server is done. The state of the server memory, cache, and other internal devices are preserved during the failover. The users do not experience an outage during this failover condition.

When the failed server is repaired and restarted, SFT II automatically resynchronizes (remirrors) the other server. For non-disruptive maintenance, SFT II can be used to shutdown one server for corrective and preventive maintenance or upgrade work while it's mirror takes-over the workload.

Note that many NetWare 5 users are considering NetWare Cluster Services, discussed later in this section.

Dynamic load/unload

NetWare's modular system architecture implementation allows the addition or removal of resource modules dynamically, while the system is operating. You can also upgrade Host Bus Adapter device drivers without shutting down the server. If you use NetWare's Hot Swap Driver capabilities, you need not even dismount disk volumes.

Client auto-reconnect

This feature automatically restores client connections when a network problem is encountered and resolved, eliminating the need for somebody from network operations to do this work. Since many network problems are intermittent and of short duration, auto-reconnect provides the appearance of application fault tolerance and availability to the end user: problems are often resolved even before the user notices them.

Kernel fault recovery or ABEND recovery

IntraNetWare 4.1x and more recent versions of NetWare can either isolate a software failure or terminate and restart the server automatically. Fault information is logged to disk for later analysis.

Novell Replication Services (NRS)

NetWare 5's Novell Replication Services (NRS) allow you to replicate data at the file level as well as at the disk level. Files, directories, applications, and Web pages can be replicated locally for redundancy, or over a WAN link to keep multiple remote sites synchronized. You can use NRS to increase network availability by deploying copies of data and applications on redundant network servers. You can also use it to achieve a form of load balancing, by strategically locating duplicate data so that it can be accessed by lesser-used network paths.

Novell Application Launcher (NAL)

System administrators can use NetWare 5's Novell Application Launcher (NAL) to centralize the management of remote users and computers. NAL can be used to add, remove or update network or desktop applications on user desktops from a central location. It can also be used to modify user desktop configuration files for personal or group applications, and to launch applications from an alternate server should a primary server become unavailable.

Hot plug PCI

Hot plug PCI is implemented in NetWare 5.x in three stages: Hot Replace, Hot Remove, and Hot Add. Hot Replace lets you replace a LAN Adapter or Host Bus Adapter without powering down the system. Hot Remove lets you remove the adapter without replacing it. Hot Add allows you to install a new adapter of a similar or different type.

Multiprocessor Kernel (MPK)

MPK provides an integrated single or multiprocessor operating system to facilitate symmetric multiprocessing (SMP)-enabled network services, thereby equipping applications to exploit the advantages of SMP. With MPK, you can scale your system, continuing to maximize availability, while protecting your investment. A new scheduling algorithm allows you to scale applications using "Fair Share" scheduling in a single or multiprocessor environment.

Intelligent I/O (I2O)

I2O provides intelligent processing on the system's input/output (I/O) channel to offload CPU processing power and make it available to applications or other host processing activities. Offloading I/O requests to an I/O processor can increase network performance, allowing a system to support more transactions and more users. In the future, I2O is expected to support direct communication between I/O devices in a clustered environment, thereby acting as a front end in processing low-level services.

Memory protection

In NetWare's memory model, system memory space and multiple protected memory spaces are kept separate. The system memory space contains the operating system code, device drivers, and processes that need to access operating system data space. NetWare Loadable Module (NLM) applications will also function in this memory space. Kernel Fault Recovery (or ABEND Recovery) protects system memory space.

The protected memory spaces can be used to run NLMs and Java Virtual Machines, providing support for cross-platform Java applets. If a process or application violates its protected memory space (by trying to write or read to a memory address outside of its assigned address space), it is automatically unloaded and the failure information logged. You can set the protected memory space to clean up and reload a process or application automatically after a failure, so users may not even experience an outage.

Flexible Mirroring, Phase I

Flexible Mirroring, Phase I allows individual disks to manage multiple NetWare partitions, so you can mirror up to four disks to a single storage disk. Drive replacement can be easily done since you're no longer required to provide two identical disks for each mirrored pair. Flexible mirroring supports availability by allowing you to manage network storage while it remains online.

Novell has also committed to introducing Flexible Mirroring, Phase II, which will allow you to mirror disk volumes without maintaining twice the mirrored storage disk space. The percentage of redundant storage space needed to maintain mirroring becomes smaller as additional storage is added to the mirrored group. This approach not only lowers the cost of mirroring, but also makes it easier to manage.

Novell Storage Services (NSS)

NSS enables high-speed access to data, applications, and network services by mounting and repairing disk volumes in seconds, regardless of volume size. This can dramatically reduce recovery time after a failure. NSS can recover quickly by tracking uncommitted storage transactions when the outage or failure occurred. It also enhances the system's ability to manage system storage resources, whether memory or disk. Finally, NSS can manage large data objects, even if they are terabytes in size or number in the thousands.

Hierarchical Storage Management (HSM)

With HSM, less frequently used files may be stored in less costly mass storage devices or removable media, such as optical drives or high-speed tape drives. HSM automates the retrieval of files as they are needed, no matter where they are stored in the hierarchy of storage devices, with the most-used data stored in high-speed magnetic disk drives.

NetWare Cluster Services (NWCS)

NetWare Cluster Services (NWCS) for NetWare 5 enables you to combine multiple NetWare servers into a cluster, giving users higher availability access to data, applications, server licenses, and other network resources. If one network server (cluster node) fails, another automatically takes over the first servers' responsibilities. NWCS cluster services allows for true multi-node clustering and can support up to 32 server nodes, on off-the-shelf Intel architecture servers.

Availability Features of Sun Solaris 8

http://www.sun.com/software/solaris/whatsnew2.html#availability

Sun Cluster

In Solaris 8, Sun Cluster software provides new and updated agents. Sun Cluster now integrates cluster functions into the Solaris kernel, and provides Java browser-based monitoring of cluster activities. It offers expanded support for servers, storage, and applications, delivering a scalable cluster solution with integrated, four-node failover support.

Solaris Resource Manager/Solaris Bandwidth Manager

Sun currently co-packages Solaris Resource Manager and Solaris Bandwidth Manager, and plans to combine them into a single product that will manage both resources and network bandwidth, via a common graphical user interface. Using these products, customers can balance computing loads across both system and network resources, maximizing both availability and quality of service.

Dynamic Reconfiguration/Automated Dynamic Reconfiguration

Dynamic Reconfiguration (DR) supports high availability hardware features, enabling systems administrators to add, change, and remove system components on a running system. Many mid-range to high-end SPARC™ systems support diverse hardware boards that can be dynamically reconfigured, such as memory and CPU boards, I/O controllers, network interface cards (NICs), disk drives, and other SCSI devices. In some instances, DR can also provide multiple paths to a single I/O controller or NIC; where this is present, Solaris 8 supports dynamic load balancing and path switching.

Automated Dynamic Reconfiguration — also known as Reconfiguration Coordination Manager (RCM) — allows you to script DR events, so your applications, databases, and management tools can act appropriately when hardware configuration or operating system events occur, without the intervention of an administrator. For example, using Automated Dynamic Reconfiguration, you might reconfigure additional CPUs and interface cards for a database server backend whenever response times fall below a level you specify.

Network multipathing

On IP networks, network multipathing lets you dynamically manage multiple links to the same network, and perform load balancing on outgoing traffic.

Live upgrades

You can upgrade to Solaris 8 or future operating systems more quickly, by building a new upgraded operating environment image while the system continues to run under a full load. You simply install Solaris software and your applications on a free disk partition using the Solaris Live Upgrade utility, then reboot to switch to the new environment. If you must revert to Solaris 7, you can do so by rebooting again.

Hot patching for diagnostics

If Sun's engineers must remotely diagnose or correct an OS bug, they can now patch most areas of the system without rebooting or interrupting operations.

Improved crash dump analysis

A new modular debugger simplifies analyzing system crash dump tapes, and can be extended using Sun's programming and scripting interfaces.

Improved program analysis

The new prstat utility, offers powerful system tuning and monitoring features similar to those in the open source top package.

Better examination of core files

In the wake of crash dumps, Solaris' system (proc) tools can now analyze process core files as well as live processes.

Bus performance monitoring

Using the new busstat tool, you can now monitor bus-related performance counters on supported SPARC platforms, measuring hardware clock cycle bus statistics such as DMA and cache coherency transactions on multiprocessor systems.

Better management of core files

The new coreadm system configuration command streamlines system-wide management of application crash (core) files, providing for flexible core file naming conventions, better management of core file locations, and better core file retention characteristics.

Improved device configuration

The new devfadm system configuration command streamlines management of special device files in the /dev and /devices directories, and supports Dynamic Reconfiguration events.

Macro-level debugging

The new apptrace application debugging tool provides call traces to Solaris shared libraries, helping application developers and support staff debug application or system problems by showing them the series of events that led to a failure.

Remote console messaging

You can now direct system events and messages to a network-connected remote console instead of the local system console.

TCP/IP network diagnostics

You can now observe TCP/IP network events and errors more easily. Solaris 8's TCP/IP protocol stack now provides internal tracing capabilities by logging TCP communications when a connection is terminated by a reset (RST) packet. When an RST is transmitted or received, information on up to ten adjacent packets is also logged.

IP packet routing observability

Solaris 8 includes traceroute, which allows network administrators to trace the route an IP packet follows to an Internet host. Traceroute is widely used to identify routing misconfiguration and path failures.

System crash dump utility

The new dumpadmn system crash dump command allows sysadmins to configure how crash dumps are captured.

Enhanced process tracing

The truss utility, which traces system calls, signals, and machine faults, can now trace the entry and exit of user-level function calls executed by the traced process.

Availability Features of AIX

Logical Volume Manager (LVM)

IBM's AIX Logical Volume Manager provides a simple and flexible mechanism for managing disk storage in AIX. Through the AIX System Management Interface Tool (SMIT), you can use LVM to perform tasks such as configuring a new disk to the system, or increasing the size of a file system or paging space while the system is online.

Disk mirroring

Disk mirroring is an LVM feature that allows a single logical file system to be associated with multiple physical copies, transparently to users and applications. If a disk, or sectors of a disk, should fail, a copy of the data can still be accessed from another disk. Mirroring improves availability by allowing the file system to remain available if disks fail, but requires extra disk drives.

AIX provides disk mirroring at a logical volume level. You can create and maintain up to three copies of a logical volume (the original and one or two mirrors). Users or applications that access files via standard AIX file manipulation routines are unaware that the files are mirrored, as AIX provides one logical view of the files.

Bad block relocation

To enhance availability, a system should handle errors on the disk surfaces. Assignment of alternative disk sectors or bad block relocation is usually done by the disk subsystem. However, the LVM is able to perform bad block relocation if the disk subsystem cannot.

Journaled File System (JFS)

AIX automatically logs all changes to a file system's structure in a logical volume called the Journaled File System log, or jfslog. Each volume group contains at least one jfslog, if there are any file systems in the volume group. At system restart, the fsck command checks the file system logs. If an error or inconsistency is discovered, the relevant journaled transactions are replayed to rebuild inconsistent file system structures.

This represents a significant departure from the methods used to recover a conventional UNIX file system. When an unplanned outage occurs, the conventional UNIX system must check the entire file system, which can be enormous. Checking the entire file system can take hours, or even days, to complete. The jfslog is a four-megabyte logical volume that contains all necessary data to correct a file system error within minutes, or even seconds. JFS significantly improves system availability by providing fast recovery from a system crash.

Dynamic AIX kernel

Traditionally, many UNIX systems management tasks have required a rebuild of the kernel or a system reboot to take effect. AIX allows many of these changes — such as an increase of page space or the addition of a new device driver, to be activated while the system is running. Avoiding the need to reboot the system for such changes increases system availability.

AIX uses less static configuration than traditional UNIX, which hardcodes many system data structures, statically binding them to the kernel. Changes to these limits require a kernel relink and a system reboot.

Tuning kernel performance is a demanding, time-consuming task. If a limit has been set too low and is exceeded in operation, the system can fail or crash. Setting limits too high, conversely, wastes system resources. AIX allocates only the resources that are needed and extends them dynamically as required. This eliminates the potential for failure because of unavailable resources, and also eliminates system administration expertise and downtime caused by kernel reconfiguration and rebuilding.

High Availability Cluster Multiprocessing (HACMP)

High Availability Cluster Multiprocessing (HACMP) for AIX® Version 4.3 allows up to 32 RS/6000 servers or SP™ nodes to be clustered, using IBM's Enhanced Scalability feature. This can greatly enhance application availability. It can also be used to support businesses with multiple locations, via IBM's RS/6000 High Availability Geographic Cluster (HAGEO), a unique disaster recovery product that delivers data redundancy and computing resources at two physical sites, no matter how far apart they may be.

System Resource Controller (SRC)

The SRC controls many AIX subsystems such as TCP/IP, NFS, SNA, and HACMP. It can automatically handle specific events, such as abnormal termination. Furthermore, the SRC provides a consistent set of commands to start, stop, trace, and query subsystem status, to facilitate their operation.

Configuration manager

At system startup, AIX automatically configures any devices added to the system. The configuration manager command, cfgmgr, can also be executed while the system is operational. This automatic capability significantly reduces the potential for error in the process of hardware configuration.

AIX update facilities

AIX allows updates to system software to be applied and tested, and then either committed or rejected. By allowing updates to be applied (not committed), you can test to ensure that the new code does not introduce problems. When you apply an update, you retain a copy of all the system files that have been superseded, so can restore them if needed. If the update causes problems, you can reject it, restoring the operating system to its previous state. Only when the update is committed, are the copies of replaced files erased.

In AIX Version 3.2, the update distribution process allowed you to install or reject selective fixes, enhancements and maintenance levels, meaning that single fixes can be applied and tested individually. For AIX Version 4, the process is essentially unchanged, apart from some new naming conventions. For example, the concept of a fileset, replaces that of an option and a subsystem. The naming convention for PTFs has also changed to a format that consists of the fileset name plus a four field, dot-separated level identifier.

Availability Features of Microsoft Windows 2000 Server and Professional

http://www.microsoft.com/windows2000/guide/platform/ overview/default.asp

Microsoft's Windows 2000 platform includes a wide range of features for maximizing availability. Many of these features are available across the Windows 2000 product family. Others are restricted to Windows 2000 Server, or to Windows 2000 Advanced Server and/or Datacenter Server, Microsoft's high-end servers. Windows 2000 features for maximizing availability are discussed in the following sections.

Windows File Protection

Ever since Windows was first introduced, a key source of problems has been the overwriting of critical system files by new applications, which often introduced system instability or incompatibilities with other applications that relied on the existing files. Windows 2000's File Protection feature prevents new software from replacing a set of system files deemed essential to Windows 2000's correct operation.

Driver certification

Another key source of system instability in earlier versions of Windows has been inadequately tested drivers. This is especially true for video drivers that run in the most privileged spaces in both Windows NT and Windows 2000. Windows 2000 introduces driver certification: only drivers that have passed Windows Hardware Quality Labs testing are included on the Windows 2000 CD-ROMs, and users are warned when they attempt to install uncertified drivers. Administrators can significantly improve Windows 2000 reliability by installing only certified drivers.

Kernel-mode write protection

Windows 2000's new kernel-mode write protection feature helps prevent errant code from interfering with system operations.

IIS application protection

In Windows 2000, Web applications run separately from the Internet Information Server 5 web server, preventing a buggy Web application from crashing the Web server and all of its applications.

Cluster services and Network Load Balancing (Advanced Server and Datacenter Server)

Windows 2000 Advanced Server supports two-node cluster services, providing automatic failover of critical applications in the event of hardware or software failure. Windows 2000 Datacenter Server extends clustering to support 4-node failover support for critical applications. Microsoft's Cluster Administrator tool can remotely control multiple Windows 2000 (and Windows NT) clusters from a single location.

Datacenter Server and Advanced Server also provide for Network Load Balancing (NLB) of clustered servers. Microsoft claims that they can redistribute the workload of a downed server in less than 10 seconds.

Windows 2000 introduces an improved, streamlined cluster services setup wizard, and integrates NLB into the Windows 2000 Advanced Server networking stack, making it possible to configure NLB without a separate installation or system reboot.

Job object API and process control

Windows 2000 Datacenter Server introduces a new extension to its process model: the job. Job objects allow administrators to manage processes, or groups of processes, to be managed and manipulated together, via Windows 2000 Datacenter Server's new Process Control tool. Administrators can finely tune the allocation of critical server resources, including processor affinity, scheduling priority, number of processes, memory usage, and CPU time, thereby improving control of operations — and potentially reducing costs by consolidating multiple applications on a single server.

Application certification & DLL protection

Microsoft now certifies applications to run on Windows 2000 Server and Professional, and Windows 2000 includes features that protect Dynamic Linked Library (DLL) files from conflicting with each other, causing application failures.

Distributed File System (Dfs)

Windows 2000's Distributed File System (Dfs) enables administrators to build a unified, hierarchical view of multiple file servers and file server shares on a network — essentially, a virtual file system. While Dfs requires substantial, careful planning, it can make it easier for users to find files, while improving availability while transparently maintaining multiple copies of files across distributed servers.

Disk quotas

You can now make the most of your storage resources, extending their life and making it easier to plan capacity, by setting disk quotas for each user and volume. Be aware, however, that users who run out of space on networked servers may resort to storing files on local PCs, where they may not automatically be backed up. If you choose to implement disk quotas, balance your policies with a realistic under-standing of your users' storage needs, and use training and education to avoid backup problems.

Hierarchical Storage Management (HSM)

Windows 2000's Hierarchical Storage Management (HSM) support enables it to automatically migrate rarely-accessed data to less expen-sive storage media, maximizing disk space for the data your users access most often.

Rolling upgrade support (Advanced Server and Datacenter Server)

Windows 2000 Advanced Server's cluster services and network load balancing features make it easier to perform rolling upgrades and planned maintenance without downtime. Using these features, you can migrate your applications or IP workload to a different node, upgrade the first node, and then migrate back. This means you can roll out server hardware, software, even OS upgrades without taking applications offline.

Dynamic Volume Management

Using Windows 2000's Dynamic Volume Management features, you can add new volumes, extend existing volumes, break or add disk mirrors, even repair RAID-5 arrays while the server remains online, transparent to users.

Error handling and protected subsystems

Windows 2000 and Windows NT Server are designed to tolerate software faults by limiting their impact on other OS components. The first line of defense against software errors is Windows 2000/NT's structured method of exception handling. When an abnormal event occurs, the event is captured and either the processor or operating system issues an exception. This design ensures that no undetected error is allowed to influence the system or other user programs.

Windows 2000 and NT Server also employ protected subsystems in their design. Protected subsystems are separate, unique memory locations that are assigned to different processes and applications. By isolating programs in this way, Windows 2000 and NT reduce the risk that a program fault will affect the system's kernel and crash the operating system. Similarly, programs are isolated from each other, so that when a program faults, it does not adversely affect other programs running on the system.

Automatic restart

All versions of Windows 2000 Server and Windows NT 4 Server can be configured to automatically restart themselves in the event of a system failure, restarting individual services, including the Internet Information Server web server.

Kill process tree

With this feature, the Windows 2000 administrator can kill every process *related* to an errant process or application, without a system reboot.

System preparation tool

For years, third-party tools such as Ghost have supported the "cloning" and rapid rollout of multiple Windows 2000 Professional workstations at once. Now, Microsoft offers a built-in tool, SysPrep, that can create an image of a computer's hard drive, including the operating system and applications, for duplication on other *identical* computers.

Windows Installer

The new Windows Installer, first introduced with Office 2000, monitors application installations and allows for cleaner, easier application uninstallation when needed. Windows 2000-certified applications must use the services of the Windows installer, though not every application you're likely to use supports it yet.

Plug and Play (PnP)

Like Windows 9x, Windows 2000 now supports "plug-and-play," automatically detecting and recognizing new hardware components, thereby simplifying network configuration and reducing downtime.

Service pack slipstreaming

Windows 2000 enables you to streamline operating system updates by maintaining a single master image of the operating system on the network that can be utilized for all upgrades.

Integrated directory services (Active Directory)

Windows 2000 introduces Active Directory, a central repository of information about all users, devices, and network elements. Properly implemented, Windows 2000 should make it significantly easier for a central IT organization to manage distributed resources, thereby lowering cost of ownership.

Active Directory uses multi-master replication to improve scalability and availability in distributed networks. Each directory replica in the network is a peer of all others. Changes made to each replica are automatically replicated across all of them.

Windows Management Instrumentation (WMI)

Windows 2000 provides a uniform model for viewing and using management data from any source. Windows Management Instrumentation (WMI) does this for applications and other software. WMI extensions to the Windows Driver Model (WDM) do much the same thing for hardware and hardware device drivers.

Delegated administration

Sites that implement Active Directory can carefully select and delegate administrative privileges to individuals throughout the organization, thereby distributing management and improving responsiveness while maintaining overall central control.

Microsoft Management Console (MMC)

Windows 2000 unifies most management tasks within a single interface, the Microsoft Management Console (MMC). Third-party management tools can also be "plugged in," making it easier to manage entire systems and networks in an integrated manner.

Windows Script Host (WSH)

Windows Script Host allows administrators to automate tasks by scripting the Windows user interface using any of several scripting languages, including VBScript and JavaScript.

Group policies and centralized desktop management

Windows 2000 group policies allow administrators to centrally manage collections of users, computers, applications, and network resources instead of managing entities on a one-by-one basis. Using group policies, administrators can control and restrict access to applications, enhance security, and perform many other tasks that would have been difficult or impossible if implemented on a desktop-by-desktop basis.

Using a variety of Windows 2000 technologies together, administrators can centrally manage users' desktop resources based on business needs and location, and provide the same desktop and data to users wherever they may travel.

Recoverable file system

Windows 2000 and Windows NT Server are designed to provide significant disk fault tolerance when running the NTFS file system. NTFS logs each disk I/O operation as a unique transaction. When a user updates a file, the Log File Service logs redo and undo information for that transaction. Redo information tells NTFS how to repeat the transaction, and undo information tells NTFS how to roll it back. If a transaction completes successfully, the file update is committed. If the transaction is incomplete or if NTFS detects an error, NTFS rolls back the transaction by following the undo instructions.

NTFS simplifies file system recovery as well. If a disk fails, NTFS can perform three passes — an analysis pass, a redo pass, and an undo pass. During the analysis pass, NTFS appraises the damage and determines exactly which clusters must now be updated per the information in the log file. The redo pass performs all transaction steps logged from the last checkpoint. The undo pass backs out any incomplete (uncommitted) transactions.

NTFS also supports hot fixing. If an error occurs due to a bad sector, NTFS moves the information to a different sector and marks the original sector as bad. This process is completely transparent to an application performing disk I/O.

Disk mirroring (RAID Level 1)

Disk mirroring is the creation and maintenance of an identical twin for a selected disk. Any file system, including FAT, HPFS, and NTFS, can take advantage of disk mirroring. Disk mirroring uses two partitions on different drives connected to the same disk controller. All data on the first (primary) partition is mirrored automatically onto the secondary partition. Thus, if the primary disk fails, no data is lost. Instead, the partition on the secondary disk is used.

Mirroring is not restricted to a partition identical to the primary partition in size, number of tracks and cylinders, and so on. This eliminates the problem of acquiring an identical model drive to replace a failed drive when an entire drive is being mirrored. For practical purposes though, the mirrored partitions will usually be created to be the same size as the primary partition.

Disk mirroring has better overall read and write performance than stripe sets with parity. Another advantage of mirroring over stripe sets with parity is that there is no loss in performance when a member of a mirror set fails. Disk mirroring, however, is more expensive in terms of dollars per megabyte because disk utilization is lower than with striping with parity. Disk mirroring is best suited for peer-to-peer and modest server-based LANs.

Disk duplexing

Disk duplexing provides a mirrored pair with an additional adapter on the secondary drive. Duplexing provides fault tolerance for both disk and controller failure. In addition to providing fault tolerance, it can also improve performance. Like mirroring, duplexing is performed at the partition level. To Windows 2000 and Windows NT 4 Server, there is no difference between mirroring and duplexing. It is simply a matter of where the other partition can be found.

Disk striping with parity (RAID Level 5)

Disk striping is another popular method of protecting data against disk failure. With disk striping, data is divided into large blocks and spread in a fixed order among multiple disks in an array. In a stripe set with parity, parity information for the data is also written across the array with the condition that the parity information and data reside on different disks. If a member of the disk array fails, data can be recovered from the parity information since it is stored on a different disk.

One advantage of stripe sets with parity is that they have better read performance (although slower write performance) than mirror sets. Another advantage is that the cost per stored megabyte is typically lower with stripe sets with parity than with mirrored sets because disk utilization is much higher.

To understand Windows 2000/Windows NT Server software-based disk striping, compare it to hardware-based striping systems. Hardware implementation of the RAID level can offer performance advantages over software implementations. With some systems, it may even be possible to replace a failed drive without shutting down the system. However, hardware RAID implementations tend to be expensive and may require an organization to lock into a single vendor solution. While offering poorer performance, software RAID is cost-effective and provides a consistent implementation across numerous hardware platforms, allowing administrators to mix and match systems for optimum price/performance.

Availability Features of IBM OS/400

In the following sections, we review selected high-availability features built into OS/400, the operating system used by IBM's AS/400 family of midrange computers.

Policy-based Backup Recovery and Management Services (BRMS)

Policy-based Backup Recovery and Management Services (BRMS) enable the AS/400 to support policy-oriented configuration and execution of backup, recovery and other operations related to removable media.

- **Centralized Management** — BRMS facilitates centralized management of media by maintaining a consistent view of removable media, its contents, location and availability across multiple AS/400 systems.

- **Hierarchical Storage Management (HSM)** — BRMS provides the AS/400 with an HSM solution that maximizes the value and performance of all storage resources. BRMS permits archiving to — and dynamic retrieval from tape, tape libraries, and save files.

Commitment control and journaling

Commitment control allows an application program to be designed so that a user must complete all changes related to a database transaction before the transaction is permanently reflected in the database. This helps ensure database integrity in the event of a system failure during a transaction. It also allows a transaction to be canceled in process if it will lead to erroneous results.

The OS/400 performs journaling, storing every database transaction in a separate file. Journaling works in conjunction with normal backup procedures to support database recovery in the event of information loss through user error or hardware failure. Recovery starts by loading an existing backup tape, then using the journal log to restore every transaction made since the last backup.

Remote journaling is now supported, offloading processing from production systems. Remote journaling enables replication on a remote AS/400 system of journals and journal receivers associated with specific local journals and journal receivers. This can reduce the time and effort needed to reconcile source and target databases following a system failure. Hot backup, data replication, and other high-availability applications can benefit from remote journaling.

System Managed Access Path Protection (SMAPP)

SMAPP is a system management feature that automatically records access path information according to mathematical algorithms set by the administrator. SMAPP allows AS/400 system administrators to tell SMAPP how long they are willing to wait for recovery to take place after a long utility outage. The system then ensures that access paths will be journaled frequently enough to achieve that recovery interval. Otherwise, they would have to manually rebuild access paths to the data in main storage before reloading it and restarting processing — a process that could take several hours.

The recovery period may be specified system-wide or by individual Application Storage Pools (ASPs). An application storage pool is a group of files related to a common set of applications. The file grouping is generally related both logically and physically.

Availability Features of Selected Hardware Components

In the following sections, we review hardware-based availability features built into a variety of leading hardware platforms.

Availability Features of IBM S/390 Integrated Server

http://www.s390.ibm.com:80/bookmgr-cgi/bookmgr.cmd/
  BOOKS/ID1TLTAB/4 percent2e0

According to IBM, the latest releases of the IBM S/390 Integrated Server mainframe offer significant reliability improvements, with MTBF improved by two to five times, depending on configuration. Using RAID disk storage can yield even better results.

High availability storage devices

The IBM S/390 Integrated Server has up to 255 Gbyte of usable disk storage internal to the system. The sixteen internal hot-swappable hard disk drives in a RAID-5 configuration allow for replacement of failing drives without a system shutdown. The system's unique cooling design promotes maximum airflow over system components and all disk drives, enhancing cooling and reliability. By reducing hardware complexity and points of failure, and by providing hot-swappable disk drives, the IBM S/390 Integrated Server delivers superior system availability.

The IBM S/390 Integrated Server model supports a RAID-5 configuration. With RAID-5, sectors that comprise a logical drive are striped across each of the hard drives in the array intermixed with parity data. In the case of disk failure, the system uses the encoded data from the surviving disks to reconstruct the lost data "on the fly." The failed disk can be replaced and automatically reconstructed during background processing on a standby disk. RAID-5 simplifies management. RAID drives can be managed together, rather than as multiple small disk drives.

RAID-5 provides high levels of data redundancy and integrity while providing excellent performance and capacity. With data "striped" across multiple high performance (7200 RPM) disk drives, normal disk I/O performance is exceptional. Depending on the specific configuration and type of workload, I/O rates as high as 400 I/Os per second can be achieved using just the internal disk storage. Should a disk drive ever fail, the system continues operating, with little degradation in performance, and the RAID subsystem recreates the missing data dynamically, as required. When the defective disk drive is replaced, the RAID-5 subsystem can rebuild the missing data onto the new drive automatically. Since the drives are all "hot-swappable," the old drive can be removed, a new drive inserted, and all data rebuilt, with no downtime or disruption.

SSA Disk: Serial Storage Architecture (SSA)

Serial Storage Architecture (SSA) offers a high performance, high availability alternative to SCSI or other older channel subsystems. SSA is an architecture that is similar in many respects to S/390 ESCON channels. It provides high data transfer rates (20 Mbytes per second) with excellent configuration flexibility and non-restrictive cable length limitations.

Since SSA disk drives are normally cabled in a loop configuration, there are two data paths to each device. Each data path is full duplex and the SSA subsystem can support four concurrent data transfers at a time. The loop configuration can continue operating when a cable or device fails. The SSA subsystem recognizes the failure and reroutes I/O requests over the remaining data path. When the failing component is replaced, the subsystem recognizes this as well, automatically reconfiguring data paths and resuming normal operation. Each SSA device has a unique, factory-assigned ID, so there are no duplicate address problems (as in SCSI) or "Master/Slave" considerations (as with EIDE).

Power management

To improve system availability, an optional Internal Battery Feature (IBF) is available. The IBF protects the system from utility outages, enabling the system to remain powered up during a short outage, and supporting an orderly shutdown in the event of an extended outage.

The power subsystem is designed with N+1 redundancy. Failure of a power thermal component does not cause a system outage. Concurrent replacement of a failed component results in an avoidance of planned outage. The power system offers dual primary (AC) power feeds, each electrically isolated, thereby enabling redundant power paths.

The combination of N+1 dual-redundant power supplies and optional internal battery backup power can virtually eliminate power-related outages. Moreover, no special power is needed. The S/390 Integrated Server uses standard power facilities (120v, 60 cycle in the US, as appropriate in other countries). As a result, installation planning and deployment costs can be minimized.

The system's built-in power monitoring continually tracks critical voltages and immediately alerts the operator if a problem occurs. If a power supply should need to be replaced, it can be "hot-plugged" without shutting down the system.

Availability Features of the IBM AS/400 Midrange System

http://www.as400.ibm.com/sftsol/hahome.htm

IBM offers the AS/400 as a highly-integrated solution for a broad range of business challenges, from delivering web services to specialized vertical market applications. A single IBM entity designs, creates, builds, tests, and services the AS/400. The same organization is responsible for hardware, operating system, database, and other middleware facilities. IBM provides support and service for the vast majority of AS/400 systems. IBM's AS/400 Development and Manufacturing teams in Rochester, Minnesota constantly track the availability of every aspect of these systems, including hardware, operating system, database, and components, and have raised average AS/400 system availability beyond 99.9%. According to IBM, customers can expect only one hardware problem every 61 months.

Logical partitions (LPAR)

Logical partitions let you run multiple independent servers — each with its own processors, memory and disks — within a single symmetric multiprocessing AS/400e. Elegant and flexible, logical partitions enable companies to reduce costs and gain competitive advantage through server consolidation.

With AS/400 logical partitions, a single AS/400 can service multiple countries. Each partition can be assigned a separate system name and may be set to run in its own national language and time zone. Companies or outsourcing vendors can run multiple independent business units in a single AS/400. Logical partitioning optimizes system resource utilization, while allowing separate accounting for IT costs for each unit.

Logical partitions allow the same AS/400e server to run both traditional interactive AS/400 business applications *and* new e-business applications, including Domino web services or business intelligence applications, tuning performance as required for each application partition.

AS/400 logical partitions also simplify the deployment of modular application suites divided between database and application servers. High performance application-to-database partition communication is supported, and new applications can be tested in test partitions without affecting production partitions.

Logical partitions can:

- Run multiple independent servers or partitions — each with its own processors, memory and disks — within a single n-way symmetric multiprocessing AS/400e

- Permit customized partition performance, allowing a single system to be fully optimized for both interactive and e-business or business intelligence workloads

- Allow each partition to be set independently, permitting different system names, languages and time zones

- Run OS/400 in each partition under a single license for the entire AS/400

- Deliver high performance inter-partition connectivity via standard LAN or WAN adapters or internally via high performance OptiConnect software — which now supports TCP/IP, enabling its use in many more applications.

Disk failure recovery

The AS/400 offers several features designed to improve disk and data reliability, and enable fast, seamless recovery from failures. These are discussed next.

- **Checksum** — A mathematical formula stores redundant information on disk in addition to business data. If a the disk unit fails, the redundant information stored on remaining disk units can be used to automatically regenerate lost information on the failed disk. While checksum increases disk storage and processing requirements, it eliminates the need to restore from backup in the event of a disk unit failure. RAID-5 controller hardware relieves the load on the central system computer for calculating the mathematical formula.

- **RAID-5, Version 4, Release 2** — Protects against failures of disk units attached to the AS/400's Multifunction I/O Processor (MFIOP) using RAID-5. The MFIOP previously only provided mirroring protection for attached disk units, but now that up to 20 disk units may be attached to it, ten can be used to provide protection. The 20 disk units are divided into two arrays of ten units, one of which is lost in each array, leaving 18 functional disk units.

- **Data Mirroring** — In data mirroring, a duplicate copy of all data is written to a second disk storage unit, which can be located on a separate disk unit controller located on a separate system bus. Data mirroring is the most expensive protection method because it requires a total duplication of not just data but the entire disk subsystem.

Of these three approaches, data mirroring offers the best reliability and least impact upon performance, followed by RAID-5, and then checksum. Data mirroring also offers performance improvements in a read-intensive database environment, because a second copy of data is always available when the first copy is busy being read by another application.

Power utility failure recovery

A power outage will rarely permanently damage an AS/400 system, but it can cause downtime. To respond, the AS/400 provides either an internal battery backup system or an interface for a Universal Power Supply (UPS). These solutions are intended primarily to protect information resident in main storage of the AS/400 system at any given time.

Usually, the internal battery backup system or UPS can supply sufficient power for a system to ride through an outage, even though the lights have gone out and user display stations have gone blank. However, longer outages are increasingly common. In fact, on average, seven outages of longer than five minutes per year will occur.

The AS/400 has been programmed to allow a certain period (changeable by the user) to pass after the first occurrence of an outage, and then to dump the contents of main storage to disk storage. This process prevents the loss of data from current applications, but may not minimize recovery time for users unless SMAPP is configured (as discussed earlier in this chapter).

Continuously Powered Main (CPM) storage

Continuously Powered Main (CPM) storage protects the main storage content in AS/400 systems with large drives. For systems capable of supporting more than 16 Gbyte of main storage, or requiring protection for more than 24 hours, an external battery unit is available.

Operations Navigator

The AS/400 is designed for office environments in which technical skills are usually limited. Operations Navigator simplifies systems management tasks, allowing administrator to use a familiar Windows-based Graphical User Interface (GUI).

Operations Navigator centralizes job manipulation, message handling, printer management, printer output handling, user and group administration, database administration, file systems, security functions, authorization lists, security and auditing policies, backup support, and hardware and software inventory. These functions may be accessed for a particular system from either a local or a remote system workstation. For example, a large company may have one AS/400 system at the headquarters location and multiple AS/400 systems distributed to other locations throughout the country or around the world. Rather than provide AS/400 and OS/400 personnel at each location, you can provide Operations Navigator to a centralized staff of help desk experts, who can coordinate with IBM's customer support structure and third-party application vendors as needed.

Operations Navigator includes support for TCP/IP configuration, including DHCP and DNS, simplified through the use of wizards. Servers can be configured to start automatically when TCP/IP is started, and server status can be monitored. Operations Navigator integrates the administration of Domino for AS/400, AS/400 NetServer software, and AS/400-based Internet services.

Plug-in Application Program Interfaces (APIs) are provided for use by other applications to integrate into the AS/400 Operations Navigator program's interface.

From the Operations Navigator window it is possible to drag and drop printer output to various printers and to the desktop, to set the Operations Navigator Windows so that the Windows can refresh their content automatically, to open separate windows to monitor specific items of interest, to create desktop shortcuts to items within Operations Navigator, and to find text within Operations Navigator lists. PC users can view and end AS/400 messages.

AS/400 system clustering

Administrators can cluster AS/400 systems (via LANs or OptiConnect links) to increase capacity and performance.

AS/400 systems support clustering across both Ethernet and IBM Token Ring networks. The use of ATM protocols makes it possible to move data in token-ring environments at up to 150 Mbps.

Instantaneous bandwidth identifies how fast data can be passed from one system in a cluster to a different system in that cluster once a connection has been established. More important is the utilization rate of the network: the proportion of instantaneous bandwidth available for information exchange between systems after accounting for resource contention, network overhead, and error recovery. On average, utilization starts to saturate for token-ring networks at 70 percent, for Ethernet at 40 percent, and for FDDI at 70 percent. LANs, though a vast improvement on wide area networks, still leave significant room for improvement.

As a result, IBM offers a second approach to clustering: the AS/400 Optical Interconnect with ObjectConnect/400. This connection can exchange data between two systems at an instantaneous data rate of 1,063 Mbps with a theoretical utilization rate of 70 percent. Furthermore, if more than three systems are in the cluster, as many as n/2 simultaneous conversations (where n is the total number of systems in the cluster) may occur concurrently, as long as the necessary data is available.

If an application needs greater performance than is available in existing systems, an additional system can be added to the clustered system network. Using parallel threads, that system will decrease the load on the existing systems, providing the performance boost that would otherwise have required the replacement of existing systems.

Clustering allows administrators to build redundancy into processing, file storage, and networking functions, using a mixture of approaches at both system and subsystem levels. Everything is transparent to the user, who needs not know which system in a cluster is executing his application.

Availability Features of the IBM RS/6000

http://www.rs6000.ibm.com/resource/aix_resource/Pubs/redbooks/ htmlbooks/sg244551.00/4551ch2.html#ssavail

Built-in error detection and correction

RS/6000 memory features single bit error correction, and double bit error detection, and the disks perform automatic bad block relocation.

Backup power supply

The RS/6000 supports an optional backup power supply, which may also perform line or power conditioning.

Battery backup systems

The RS/6000 supports battery backup systems that can sense the failure of external power and switch to battery-supplied power, providing a limited amount of time for orderly shutdown.

A customizable system interface to the power supply's electronics is provided to shut down the system gracefully as the battery nears the end of its power. Advanced warnings of an impending shutdown not only reduces recovery time, but also warns users to save their work and complete their jobs. If power returns before the shutdown of the system, the system switches back to regular power and continues working without interruption. Meanwhile, the battery begins to recharge itself to prepare for the next power failure.

Rack-mounted RS/6000 models provide an optional Battery Backup Unit with 1500 watts of standby power, which can keep a system operating on battery power for at least ten minutes.

Redundant or spare disks

To increase system availability, the RS/6000 supports installation of redundant or spare disks. Mirroring, in effect, provides this capability automatically. Nevertheless, a spare disk could also be added to a system to provide a backup for any failed volumes. This technique is particularly valuable in installations that are distant from service locations, or are serving especially critical applications.

Hot-pluggable disk drives

Hot-pluggable disk drives allow replacement of failed units while a system remains online. While this improves system availability, the data contained on the failed disk must be copied to the replacement, either from a backup, from a mirrored copy, or through the use of RAID parity disks.

The RS/6000's 9333 Serial Disk Drive Subsystem supports drive replacement without powering down the system. Its self-docking, pluggable design eliminates the need to physically connect cables. The power supply provides a separate port to each disk with over-voltage and current protection to maximize safety during maintenance.

Multi-tailed disks and shared volume groups

Multi-tailed disks are disks that are cabled to two or more separate system units. The data contained on a given disk is usually accessed exclusively by a single system. Concurrent data access by multiple systems is considered a specialized implementation. Also known as disk-sharing or bus sharing, concurrent data access enables the RS/6000's High Availability Cluster Multiprocessing (HACMP) feature to take over a disk resource from a failed system.

RAID disk arrays

As discussed elsewhere in this chapter, RAID provides improved availability, security and performance over conventional disk systems. While appearing logically to the operating system as a single disk drive, a RAID array is actually made up of several disks, which have their data spread across the drives in a variety of methods designed to improve performance, reliability, or both.

Availability Features of Compaq Proliant Servers

http://www6.compaq.com/enterprise/highavailability.html

Intel-architecture servers from a variety of leading vendors now offer significant high availability features. In this section, we review several representative features offered by Compaq, one of the industry's leaders. These features include ECC memory, SMART-2 Array Controller Technology with RAID support and On-Line Capacity Expansion, component redundancy, and the Recovery Server Option.

ECC memory

Compaq has incorporated ECC (Error Checking and Correcting) memory in all of its servers to improve the data integrity and, therefore, prevent data from being corrupted or lost while being processed in memory. Many Compaq Proliant servers feature an ECC-protected processor bus for even further protection.

SMART-2 Array Controller technology

Because storage is one of the most critical elements in a high-availability server, fault management is critical. Compaq's SMART-2 Array

Controller technology not only supports RAID functionality but also offers On-Line Capacity Expansion, which allows pluggable hard drives to be added to a configuration without disrupting server operation. During expansion, ECC memory and battery backup of the enhanced array accelerator prevent potential outages that might be caused by memory or power failures.

Redundant network interface cards

Since network connectivity is crucial for servers, Compaq servers support a second PCI network controller to be installed for standby use. If the active controller fails, the standby controller assumes operation without loss of service, eliminating a key single point of failure.

Uninterruptible Power Supply

To guard against external power outages and accommodate inconsistent power, Compaq offers the Uninterruptible Power Supply (UPS). This power supply has an enhanced level of protection that not only prolongs its own battery life, but also monitors the battery's condition to identify an impending failure in advance.

Compaq Insight Manager

Server management software can effectively identify and even predict faults before they cause a disruption in system operation. Compaq Insight Manager is a key component of an overall systems and network management approach that provides in-depth fault, configuration, and performance monitoring of Compaq hardware. Through these management capabilities, Insight Manager helps predict component failures so preventive maintenance can be performed, and identifies faults when they do occur. Additionally, it can provide performance management of all major subsystems to keep them running at peak levels. It can also run remote server diagnostics to isolate faults, carry out server reconfiguration, and restart the remote server if needed.

Standby Recovery Server

Compaq also offers multi-server configurations called Recovery Server Options. The Standby Recovery Server, the first mode of the option, is a failover solution connecting two Compaq servers that share a common set of Proliant Storage Systems. One server acts as a standby for the other. In the event that the primary server fails, a switchover will be initiated and the standby server will take over the operation. The disk storage connected to the failed server is automatically switched to the secondary server, which restarts, bringing the system back online within minutes. This automated process provides recovery without administrative intervention and the ability to service a failed server when it is most convenient.

On-Line Recovery Server

On-Line Recovery Server, the second mode of Compaq's Recovery Server Option, is a failover implementation that pairs two Compaq servers to provide backup services for each other. Unlike the Standby Recovery Server configuration, each server, during normal operation, can perform independent tasks. The two servers typically do not share Proliant Storage Systems. In the event of a server failure, the surviving server takes over the load of the failed server in addition to maintaining its own load. Thus, it is crucial that the surviving server has enough power and memory to accommodate the additional workload.

Rapid recovery

To minimize the impact of failures in software, memory, processor and even a system's environment, Compaq has implemented rapid recovery features in all of its servers. Automatic Server Recovery-2 (ASR-2) and Server Health Logs work in conjunction to recover a server to its state prior to the error. If an error occurs in one of the subsystems, ASR-2 logs the error in the Server Health Logs, attempts to restart the system, and takes other necessary action, such as deallocating bad memory to avoid subsequent faults.

Redundant power supply

To prevent power supply failures from causing system outages, Compaq offers a redundant power supply option that duplicates the functions of the internal power supply, minimizing the risk of interrupted service.

Off-line backup processor

An off-line backup processor option can alleviate the outage risks associated with processor failure. A system containing multiple processors can automatically be powered down, reconfigured, and restarted from the second processor, minimizing interruption of system operation. If the operating system supports multiprocessing, the off-line backup processor can be used not only for backup purposes but for processing also.

External storage

The Compaq Proliant Storage System can address the need for external storage that requires fault-tolerant capability and expandability. This storage system supports hot-pluggable drives and intelligent RAID array controllers for various levels of fault tolerance.

▶ Availability Features of Selected Software Components

Availability Features of the Oracle8i Database

Increasingly, enterprise software packages have their own high availability features. As an example, this section reviews the high availability features associated with one of the leading enterprise database systems, Oracle8i.

The Oracle8i database and Oracle8i Parallel Server incorporate features aimed at achieving higher scalability and availability for On-Line-Transaction-Processing (OLTP) and Internet applications.

Cache Fusion clustering

Oracle's Cache Fusion technology uses dedicated high-speed interconnects and Oracle Parallel Server's new ability to pass data directly between nodes to create unparalleled application scalability. Cluster load balancing dynamically connects users to a system node in the cluster that is least utilized, reducing the time the user waits to access information, and increasing the number of users that can be served.

Oracle8i also makes clustering technology feasible for more companies by eliminating the need for application customization. In the past, many applications needed to be custom-tailored to use clustering technology, but with Cache Fusion most applications can transparently scale.

Fast-Start architecture

Fast-Start architecture improves recovery time from system faults by nearly 5000 percent by providing fast and predictable recovery from faults. In Oracle's testing, recovery time was reduced from 15 minutes to 17 seconds using Fast-Start. Coupled with Oracle8i's transparent application failover capability that automatically reconnects applications to the database, outages are masked from the users.

Online reorganization

Online reorganization allows database maintenance to be done while the user or customer is accessing the data. Users can reorganize tables, partitions, and indexes without taking the database offline. These new online Oracle8i maintenance capabilities improve data availability, query performance, response time, and disk space utilization.

Single system view

Single system view simplifies cluster management by making an entire cluster of servers appear as one system to the administrator. This approach reduces the complexity of administration and maintenance, minimizing human error. It also reduces the time and effort needed for system maintenance and backup, making larger clusters not only possible but practical.

Index